ARISE FROM DARKNESS

FR. BENEDICT J. GROESCHEL, C.F.R.

Arise from Darkness

WHEN LIFE DOESN'T MAKE SENSE

IGNATIUS PRESS   SAN FRANCISCO

Cover art: John Lynch
"*Arise from Darkness:*
The Cross Stands Firm While the World Turns"
Cover design: Riz Boncan Marsella

To Our Lady of Sorrows
and her children
who have taught me so much

Contents

Acknowledgments

I am very grateful to all who over the years have indirectly helped me write this book by their example of courage and merciful love in the face of great difficulties. I am grateful also for the spiritual writers who have helped me to go on in the challenges of life and whom I have mentioned in this book.

Thanks to a friend who wishes to remain anonymous for typing the manuscript, and to Barbara Valenzuela of the staff of St. Augustine's Cathedral in Tucson, Arizona, who helped with the final touches. I am also grateful to Catherine Murphy, our secretary at Trinity, for generously helping and to John Lynch for another powerful painting for the cover. Thanks go also to Sister Catherine Walsh of the staff of St. Joseph's Seminary Library, Dunwoodie, and to David Burns, also of St. Joseph's, for proofreading.

I want to acknowledge the kindness of Doubleday and Tan Publishers for permission to use longer passages from the works of Père de Caussade, and of Templegate for permission to use quotations from its editions of the writings of Julian of Norwich.

Finally, I am deeply grateful to all who pray for me and my work, especially to Sister Mary of the Presentation of the Blessed Sacrament Sisters in Yonkers, New York, who has me at the top of her prayer list and who, in the past, has helped me so often to arise from darkness.

Fr. Benedict J. Groeschel, CFR
St. Crispin Friary
Bronx, New York
Palm Sunday, 1995

I

Arise from Darkness

The young woman who sat a few feet from me quietly wept tears that indicated an unspeakable inner desolation. A week before, her husband had been killed in what is called a "freak accident", leaving her with two small children and an empty life. On his way to work on Wall Street he had been struck by a piece of falling masonry that inexplicably had become dislodged from a well-kept building. The insurance companies sometimes refer to such things as "acts of God".

The couple had had a good marriage despite all the challenges of starting a new family. They were, in fact, "two in one flesh". Half of her life had been torn away from her in an instant. Her two little children—a boy of three and a girl of five—looked on, not really comprehending that they would never see their daddy again. Friends, and there were many, tried to say something consoling, but really did not know what to say. The husband's parents and family were overwhelmed in their own grief, and her family looked on hopelessly, trying to make some sense out of what was senseless. The priest who preached at the funeral had really done his best; he had been quoted in the local newspapers. He had directed everyone's attention to Christ's promise of eternal life. His fellow clergy of all denominations who read about the funeral were thankful to God that they did not have to preach.

After the funeral the vast majority of mourners, who were genuinely compassionate and "felt very bad about what happened", went on with their own lives. Very close members of the family committed themselves to various kinds of help, but even their lives went on. The young widow remained in her darkness. Every place in her home became haunted by memories. Objects filled with meaning and joy became crowns of thorns—the wedding picture, his favorite coffee mug, his yearbook. Breakfast, which they used to share so early before he walked to the train, became an almost unendurable reliving of that last breakfast and then the call later from the police. She did not even want to go to her parish church because it brought back scenes of the funeral; she did not want to meet the priest who had come over to the house when he got the news and who had preached the funeral sermon that she could not even remember because she had not really heard it.

You who read these lines are moved even as you read them because you know that they could have been written about you with a few details changed. These lines are written about you . . . and they are written about me. They are written about us all.

Why Did God Do It?

The clergy and lay ministers of every denomination hear this question so often and cannot really answer it. We run away from it because usually it is not a question but a cry of pain in the form of a prayer that is half bewilderment and often tinged with rage. As we will see, this outraged cry to the mysterious God is often the most sincere and attentive prayer that many people ever offer.

I recall driving past a suburban home and stopping because there were police cars, an ambulance, and neighbors standing around looking at the house. I inquired of a lady wearing an apron what had happened, and she said between sobs, "Crib death—the first child." The name on the mailbox was Italian, and I asked if a priest had come yet. She said no, so I parked and went in. In the midst of great confusion, a young woman was being consoled by relatives and older women who were embracing and kissing her. When she saw me in my friar's robes, she jumped up and grabbed me around the neck so hard that she ripped my robe down the front as she cried out, "Why?" This was not a question. It had no answer that I could ever possibly give. I knew even then that the horror of this hour would pass, that she would calm down, that she might very well have other children. But the question would remain for the rest of her life, "Why?"

I will not try to answer that question. I don't think that the human mind is or ever will be large enough to give a satisfactory answer to these questions: Why does evil occur? Why did the God who made the world so beautiful permit it to be scarred with such terrible wounds? Why does God, who is light, permit such darkness?

Beginning a Half Century Ago

The writing of this book began more than a half century ago when the first great tragedy came into the life of a little boy. Since his father built defense plants during World War II, he attended more than a dozen grammar schools in as many places. This boy, named Peter, had two faithful companions who went with the family wherever they were transferred. Often this meant transferring twice in a single school year, leaving behind the beginnings of friendships that could not develop in so short a time. These two faithful friends were Scottish terriers, a mother and daughter, and they died within a few months of each other, leaving the little boy bereft and in deep mourning. Don't smile. Often for people who are left alone by circumstances or personality traits, a pet becomes an important companion in life. For a child, the death of a pet can be a deep wound similar to the loss of a human being. I remember praying for these Scotties and asking in my loneliness: Why, why did God take them away from me?

Since then, like all little children who grow up, I have lived through worse tragedies, and all that time this book has been growing inside of me, because a real book is a living thing, a tree that will bear fruit in due time. As I have said, I don't think that one can find in this world a completely satisfying answer to the question "Why?" There will be an answer in eternity when our minds will be large enough to deal with the mystery of evil because "we shall be changed" (1 Cor 15:51).

A Guide—Not an Answer

This book is not an answer but a guide to those in darkness. It is about going on in spite of darkness, about survival, and about using the unavoidable dark times of life to grow. There is actually nothing new in what I suggest. The solution, not the answer, that I will try to enunciate is found in the gospel and in the lives of great saints, heroes and heroines, and in the lives of very brave ordinary people whom we all have known. Many guides have been written for people struggling with the mystery of evil. It is the theme of much of the great literature of the human race. But in each generation the question returns; each age has its own dark background in front of which the struggle to keep going and find meaning must be worked out. In every age, men, women, and children not only ask "Why?" but ask "How am I going to go on to arise from darkness?" It is that which my book will address.

The artwork for the cover of this book was created by John Lynch, who has done several paintings for my books. He tells me that it was done quite spontaneously at a time of darkness for him. The painting came unplanned and unprepared for. It depicts a woman blinded by pain, destruction, and confusion. The figure stands, a sign of determination to go on even when the reasons for survival are obscure, in the blindness of the moment. In the heart of the woman there is a light marked by a Cross—a sustaining belief, a truth to be found in the sufferings of Christ. In the background is a vision of the heavenly city. Like all such visions, it is only a symbol of a reality transcending all human images. John also proposed the title of this book drawn from the painting, *Arise from Darkness*. That is what the figure is doing and what we all must struggle to do with the help of the divine grace shining in our inmost being.

As we shall see, the Christian response to the problem of evil and suffering began with the Cross of Christ. A Christian cannot find an answer apart from the Cross—apart from Jesus' own encounter with evil and his triumph over it, his rising from darkness. This response is the struggle to hope. But how? But where? But why? In these reflections I have tried to recall some of the most frequently encountered sorrows and griefs: the failure of friends, financial and personal insecurity, the failure of the Church, our own inconsistent behavior and self-destructiveness, the death of loved ones, and the inescapable loss that we all experience when all that we rely on in this world is slipping away from us. The consideration of each of these painful experiences offers opportunities for us to examine them in the light of our faith in Christ. What is more important, we will be able to learn from the experiences of others how they have learned to rise from darkness by the strength of faith and hope.

I will draw lessons from the lives of people I have known or heard about. When necessary to protect the identity of these people I will alter the details but never the essentials of what has happened to them. This is done to protect those who do not need to have their wounds opened again. Some whom I have contacted have given me permission to use their experiences and even their words undisguised.

Who Should or Should Not Read This Book?

Some readers may be saying to themselves: "This is too heavy for me right now. Things are going fairly well, and I hope they will continue to go well." If you feel that way, don't read this book now. Put it aside for a day when you may need it. Others will say: "Things are going well for me now, but I would like to be compassionate to others, to share their grief even though my life is fairly tranquil." You may wish to share this book with someone now in the incredible darkness that eventually comes upon us all.

However, this book is written expressly for those going through a time of darkness and pain. I have tried to look at the question "Why?", and I have found only partial answers. I am convinced that believers who are unafraid to pay the price will know what to do though they are unable to understand why this is all happening. The *what* is much more likely to be found than the *why* is to be answered.

The *what* cannot be said in a sentence or a few paragraphs. It is experienced in the single intuition of the Cross, the vision of Calvary and the Resurrection, but this vision must be drawn out into words and applied to the difficult situations that are likely to cause darkness and pain. Picture yourself at night in a dark wood; far ahead of you is a light. Everything else is darkness. There is no doubt about what way to go—toward the light. But between you and the light there is unknown terrain—ditches, brambles, perhaps a barbed wire fence. How do you find the way to the light? You are exhausted, frightened, inclined just to sit there in the dark in hopes that the sky will lighten. You can just wait.

But if you are moved to challenge the darkness, to arise, to follow the light, to find the way, to move on with the precious time of life, then this book is written for you.

The First Step—Getting over the Big Lie

There is an incredible untruth communicated to children as they grow up in our technologically advanced world, namely, that most people have a good chance of living out their lives without times of suffering or pain, times of darkness. This illusion is created by the media, especially by advertising (a world of happy endings), by education, by generalized attitudes that make up the social customs of our people, and even by our religious thinking. Everyone's life is supposed to be filled with sunshine; and when it is not, luck will change, things will work out well, and the sunny carefree times will return. Not to worry—all will be roses.

This untruth is not a deliberate lie—in fact it is the universal denial of reality. It is not a deception to be condemned but an illusion to be dispelled. We must do this if we are ever to arrive at any mature sense of relative peace and security in this world. Every person reading these lines will have had some real experiences of darkness in life already, and all will have more unless they die soon. Many are in darkness now, and that's why they have picked up this book. If one does not face this very obvious fact—that times of suffering, pain, and difficulty are inevitable—one will run neurotically through life like a frightened animal. One is likely to become disillusioned and deeply depressed or cynical or filled with a brooding anger. Very likely this anger will be aimed at God; he should have made the world a better place.

If we do not run away from trouble or attempt to avoid it completely, then what are we to do? Obviously the first thing is to have a conviction, a mindset, that trouble and pain are inevitable parts of life. They come to all, especially to those who try desperately to protect themselves from suffering. The most bitterly disappointed people are those who thought that this brief, fragile life was going to bring them the joy reserved for the blessed in heaven.

Once you have rejected the illusion that life is really delightful for most people (and you hoped to be included among them), then you are prepared to face dark times. Some decide to do this by a stoic determination, generally maintaining a dignified silence and trying to avoid involving others in their pain. This attitude may lead to a certain maturity, but it can also lead to a quiet hopelessness, a humorless and bleak approach to life. A stoical friend of mine described life as a journey from obscurity to oblivion. This appraisal omits an appreciation of our own eternal vocation, which brings us beyond the sorrows of this world.

This stoical attitude is deeply entrenched in the social customs of northern European people and their cousins abroad in North America, Australia, and New Zealand. It also seems to be noticeable in Japan and in the upper class of India. For these people, technological progress is supposed to make pain unnecessary and suffering an aberration. Therefore, to admit suffering becomes socially unacceptable.

"A stiff upper lip" in time of life's pain and disappointments makes our relationships with our neighbors superficially more pleasant. However, it is worth observing that the nations I have mentioned are not only characterized by a denial of their sorrow but are also the places where neurosis and the psychotherapy that it requires, now that psychotherapy has become a panacea, are most common. I read somewhere recently that psychotherapy moves people from being miserable to being unhappy. Pretense, denial, and repression are all causes of the neuroses that are so characteristic of the so-called "first world". The only nations in the West appearing to avoid this neurotic stoicism and pretense are the Latin nations. You may remember, if you are old enough, immigrant relatives who were not yet smitten by the denial of the first world. They told you how they really felt when you asked them.

The obvious fact is that everyone suffers and that almost all go through periods of deep suffering and darkness. Some, inexplicably, seem to experience more suffering than others. If you are in darkness, recognize the fact that you have plenty of company. If you have failed to admit the universal human experience of suffering, then this recognition should make you more compassionate and sensitive to people's hidden pain in the future. By rejecting the unwarranted illusion that "everyone is doing well but me", you will become a far more open human being, sensitive to the sufferings of others, and willing to listen and help. What is far more important, you will not look on this Christian way of acting as a chore or burden. Even if things are going well, compassionate concern for others will constantly remind you that life is not always sunshine. In a wounded world marked by the mystery of the original fall of the human race, life cannot always be beautiful, but it can be filled with meaning.

To Arise Means to Go Beyond

It is not enough merely to survive the trials of life; it is necessary to go beyond them. In the moment of unforeseen grief (like the profound and sudden sorrow of the two young women I mentioned above), any thought of growing through pain is usually incomprehensible. The suggestion alone may cause anger and be resisted. But the intense anger, which is a predictable response to threat, will give way to a decision to go on, to live with the sorrow and even to grow from it. This is what the saints mean by the mystery of the Cross, a mystery essentially linked to the Resurrection. Just as Easter is meaningless without Calvary, Calvary is incomprehensible without the victory of the empty tomb.

If you are reading this book in the intense moment of grief, you need to discipline yourself just to hold on, to survive mutely and without understanding why. But if your suffering has subsided a bit and you have lived with it for a time and are trying to take up your responsibilities to others, to put the pieces back together, you need to ponder the mystery of the Cross. The message of the death and Resurrection of Christ is this: with faith we can go repeatedly on in this life by using defeat and loss as an opportunity to challenge God's grace to help us survive. In Genesis 32, Jacob wrestled with the angel of God in the darkness. Although wounded and limping, he received the blessing and went on

his way. St. Paul's boast amid his sufferings and disappointments expresses so well the mystery of the Cross (2 Cor
11:21–12:10). All we have to be proud of, to claim as our
own, is our weakness and failures, but we can boast "in the
Cross of our Lord Jesus Christ" (Gal 6:14). When we are
knocked down and defeated by life, abandoned by friends,
betrayed by those we thought we could rely on, weary of
our own foolishness or even facing death, that is when we
can pick up the Cross and wave it at grief, sadness, and
death. To boast in the Cross, it seems to me, is an almost
fierce gesture when we confront all that would defeat us and
say: "Look at the Cross, all of you, and know that I shall not
be overcome, because the Lord of Life is with me and in me,
and he will go with me even through the valley of the
shadow of death."

The following words of the gentle English mystic and an-
choress Blessed Julian of Norwich[1] sum this up so well.
Speaking of Christ she wrote:

> Though we are in such pain, trouble and distress, that it seems
> to us that we are unable to think of anything except how we
> are and what we feel, yet as soon as we may, we are to pass
> lightly over it, and count it as nothing. And why? Because God
> wills that we should understand that if we know him and love
> him and reverently fear him, we shall have rest and be at peace.
> And we shall rejoice in all that he does.
>
> I understood truly that our soul may never find rest in things
> below, but when it looks through all created things to find its
> Self, it must never remain gazing on its self, but feast on the
> sight of God its maker who lives within.
>
> He did not say, "You shall not be tempest-tossed, you shall
> not be work-weary, you shall not be discomforted." But he

[1] Julian of Norwich, *Enfolded in Love: Daily Readings with Julian of Norwich*,
trans. a Member of the Julian Shrine [from *Exeter Medieval Texts*, chap. 65, 67,
68, ed. Marian Glasscoe] (London: Darton, Longman and Todd, 1980), 39.

said, "You shall not be overcome." God wants us to heed these words so that we shall always be strong in trust, both in sorrow and in joy.

— *Prayer* —

LORD JESUS CHRIST, long ago at baptism I became your child and disciple. I have often, as best I was able, recommitted myself to following after you, in spite of all my inconsistencies and failures. I am very weak and confused, and when darkness comes into my life I feel discouraged, overcome, rejected by you. I feel myself to be a scavenger along the debris-filled highways of life. I forget that most if not all of my fellow travelers at some time experience the same feelings, the same painful trials.

Be with me in the dark time, and give me, please, some sign, some awareness of your presence. Send me a ray of hope when the road is long and weary and I feel all alone. At least send your Holy Spirit that I may know in some way you are still with me when all is dark. Amen.

2

When Friends Fail

In the Gospel of John we read these most sorrowful words of the Savior at the Last Supper: "The hour is coming, indeed it has come, when you will be scattered, every man to his home, and will leave me alone" (16:32). Jesus is speaking to his disciples and predicting that, despite their protestation of loyalty to him, they are all about to leave him alone. Why did Jesus Christ experience the absence, the betrayal, the failure of his friends? How could they have failed him? Why did they do this to one who had been so good to them? Many Christian writers have seen that in his Passion, Christ endures every suffering, every pain, every humiliation, every sorrow that can come to human beings. As a result Christ must suffer even this—to be betrayed by his friends, to be left alone. This he must endure so that we will know that God has taken upon himself all human pain and suffering.

The experience of having friends fail comes to us all. This most painful experience of life can include the loss of family, parents, spouses, and children, as well as dear friends. Suddenly we are left alone. I am not implying that these loved ones fail us on purpose or that they are necessarily at fault. Many times friends fail to be there for us simply because they are human. Perhaps they have died. We desperately need them, and they are not there because death has taken them away. There isn't an adult who doesn't know what I am writing about. We long for the support on which we relied from loved ones, and they're gone. If we have a strong, sturdy faith we can say, "Oh, yes, they are praying for me on the other side", and we're right. But you can't sit down and have a cup of coffee with them. You can't call them on the phone and say, "What a day!"

And people fail us for other reasons. First of all, friends change and we change. Did you ever sit down and count all the friends that you've lost simply because they changed or you changed? Often, at an AA meeting (I'm an honorary alcoholic), I've heard people say, "I joined AA, and the first thing I realized is that I'd lost all my drinking buddies." That's why AA quickly comes to the rescue (as do the other twelve-step programs) with a whole new set of friends.

In all circumstances of life, friends change. It's no one's fault. My best friend in high school also became a priest, but he's changed; he's no longer a priest. We meet every few years, catch up on things, but our lives are incredibly different—our goals and purposes are far apart. Then, I opened a photo album one day. I was looking at a picture of Mother Teresa at our retirement home. We were at Benediction of the Blessed Sacrament. Kneeling next to me was a young priest I had known very well as a seminarian, a friend—and he's gone, he's changed. We all change. Our interests change. Our desires change. Our energies change. If you live to be quite on in years, you may lose track of your friends, simply because you've become old, and they are old. No one remarks, "We're not going to see you again until the other side", but we know that this is likely to be our last meeting on earth. Things change, people move away, circumstances arise, and change takes place. What was once very meaningful is gone, swept away by the tide of time.

Sometimes we lose our friends and relatives because of competitiveness or hurt feelings. We live, unfortunately, in a very competitive society. Consequently, it's a world of jealousy where children are told, "You have to get ahead; you have to win." There's always a race, a contest, or something, even if it's not announced as a competition. And sometimes we win and lose a friend in the process, or they win and lose us. Frequently all of this is unrecognized and is no one's fault, but it is everyone's loss.

The loss of friends is most painful in family relationships. Children grow up together. They enjoy everything together; they suffer, weep, laugh, and play together, and the years go on. In this age brothers and sisters may live on different continents, worlds apart. They meet years later, and they hardly know each other. In a certain sense, we can say that there once was a friendship and now it's gone, leaving just a biological relationship. If you add to competitiveness the disputes over property and inheritances or simple jealousy, then you can understand how what was once a family becomes simply a festering wound. What was once a bond of love becomes a chain of hate.

We lose loved ones also because of resentment. We all want to be loved in a special way, and sometimes our relatives, even our closest relatives, or our best friends don't love us in the special way that we think we need. And why do we need that? Because we're self-centered. We have no right to be so special in the way that we demand, but when we don't get this desired special attention we turn away.

We lose our friends also because God calls us to do something different. Some have lost their friends and families because they've gone through a religious conversion or, on the other hand, because they've lost their faith. Religious faith binds people together, but it also separates them. Some believe they have been called to take a way different from the rest of their friends and relatives.

I know a sister who left her own community after about twenty years there and joined another one where she felt called. It was painful for her and for them. I told her that I know how she felt. It happened to me. I have confrères who were friends of mine for half a lifetime and who feel now that I walked out on them.

The day we left our former community, I read an essay by Cardinal Newman called "The Parting of Friends". Newman wrote this essay when he was leaving the Anglican Church to bid farewell to his closest friends. He belonged to that remarkable group called the Oxford Movement. This was a circle of about twenty friends who in many ways changed the Anglican Church and most of the Christian churches in the English-speaking world, including the Catholic Church. Some of them became Catholics, some didn't. Dr. Pusey and John Keble were close friends of Newman who remained Anglicans. And Newman was someone who loved friendship. He said he considered it the greatest blessing of his life that he had had good friends. But he had lost his very best friends. The following paragraph gives you some insight into Newman's pain and their pain. The "any one" he refers to is himself.

> And, O my brethren, O kind and affectionate hearts, O loving friends, should you know any one whose lot it has been, by writing or by word of mouth, in some degree to help you thus to act; if he has ever told you what you knew about yourselves, or what you did not know; has read to you your wants or feelings, and comforted you by the very reading; has made you feel that there was a higher life than this daily one, and a brighter world than that you see; or encouraged you, or sobered you, or opened a way to the inquiring, or soothed the perplexed; if what he has said or done has ever made you take interest in him, and feel well inclined towards him; remember such a one in time to come, though you hear him not, and pray for him,

that in all things he may know God's will and at all times he may be ready to fulfil it.[1]

The Recognition of Friends

Sometimes we recognize real friends only when they are departing or are already gone. I had a bittersweet experience recently. One of the fine priests of the New York Archdiocese, Fr. James McGuire, pastor of St. John and Mary Church in Chappaqua, was dying. We weren't close friends, but we were friendly acquaintances. And I had given him a number of retreats. His nickname was "Gentleman Jim", because he was always rather proper, a little bit reserved, but friendly and very intelligent. He was always grateful for what you did for him. The deacon in the parish kindly called me and said, "Jim would like to see you, and he is close to death." When I arrived at the rectory, I saw that he had a very bad cancer on the side of his face. His jaw was held in place by a support. We had the most beautiful and precious visit. Sickness had made him less reserved and more spontaneous. When I and the novice who came with me were leaving, the novice asked for Father's blessing, and Jim gave us a beautiful, long, heartfelt blessing. When we stood up, he said, "You know, it shows you what suffering will do. I gave you the 'Protestant blessing'." (We used to call "In the name of the Father and of the Son and of the Holy Ghost" the Catholic blessing; but when we made up a spontaneous blessing for the occasion, we called it the "Protestant blessing" because ministers are accustomed to giving this type of blessing.) Jim was so open, so revealing

---

[1] John Henry Newman, *Sermons Bearing on Subjects of the Day*, Sermon 26 (New York: Longman, Green, 1902), 395.

of his feelings, and he said something to me that was really very beautiful. He said, "You know, Ben, I've been up and down three times with this thing" (referring to the cancer), "and each time I went down, he came with me. And each time I came up, he came with me. And I know he will go with me when the time comes for me to leave." Now, for a quiet, reserved man, this was extremely revealing. I hadn't seen Jim for a few years, but in the crucible of suffering shared, many things had become possible. Defenses were moved away. We were honest and not simply conventional.

How really hidden we all are from each other. "How are you?" "Oh, fine." We could be dying and we would say, "Oh, fine." When you are with the poor and you ask someone, "How are you?" and he's dying, he says, "I'm dying. I'm scared." In the suburbs when you ask, "How are you?" he says, "Oh, I'm fine. I have cancer of the brain, but I'm fine." We are usually afraid to tell even our friends the truth about ourselves because we are afraid to lose them. My friend Msgr. Bob Brown passed away a few years ago, but he was different. He was very ill and lived for six years with cancer. If you asked him, "Bob, how are you?" the answer would be, "Great, for a guy who is dying of cancer." The first time he said this I was speechless. We're afraid to share the very things that would bring others closer to us and us closer to them. We are afraid to share our sufferings. We might recall that our Lord Jesus Christ was not afraid to share his sufferings. He still shares them. That's what a crucifix is about.

The Loss of the Son of God

Separation from loved ones and friends is, then, something that happened to the Son of God. Think of the Son of God, the second Person of the Trinity, as a Divine Person, not yet son of Mary, but simply Son of God. He existed as Son from all eternity. Before he came into this world he was called by an unspeakable name that we render as "The Son of God; The Only Begotten Son". He lived in this incredible, unthinkable relationship with the heavenly Father and the Holy Spirit. We have only the vaguest awareness of this, but what we do understand is that out of all eternity there was a relationship. The God Who Is was not alone. He was not an isolated thinking mind by itself. But there was a Divine Intelligence and Being with Three Persons. This is an utter mystery. People sometimes say to me, "What difference does the Trinity make?" It makes all the difference in the world about how you think of relationships, because there *was* one out of all eternity. The Son left that relationship in some incomplete way and came to earth. The Gospel of St. John puts it very colorfully in Greek, "He pitched his tent among us" (Jn 1:14). (To "pitch one's tent" is the idiomatic expression in Greek for living near someone.) He came with us. He profoundly experienced being separated, although He was at the same time always mysteriously united with the Father.

Without attempting to summarize the many valuable commentaries and theological writings on his coming among us, we shall pause to meditate for a moment on these lines to catch some echo of the separation of the Son of God from his Father. This separation happened when the Son of God came and, as the child of Mary, lived among us for the three decades of his earthly life.

> Have this in mind among yourselves, which was in Christ Jesus, who, though he was in the form of God, did not count equality with God a thing to be grasped at, but emptied himself, taking the form of a servant, being born in the likeness of men. And

being found in human form he humbled himself and became
obedient unto death, even death on a cross (Phil 2:5–8).

The true light that enlightens every man was coming into the
world. He was in the world, and the world was made through
him, yet the world knew him not. He came to his own home,
and his own people received him not. But to all who received
him, who believed in his name, he gave power to become children of God; who were born, not of blood nor of the will of
the flesh nor of the will of man, but of God. And the Word
became flesh and dwelt among us, full of grace and truth; we
have beheld his glory, glory as of the only Son from the Father
(Jn 1:9–14).

Along with his separation from his Father, Jesus experienced the failings and shortcomings of his human friends.
His boyhood acquaintances and friends in Nazareth at-
tempted to kill him. These were his neighbors in a small,
isolated country town. Many of them were related to him.
They took him to the brow of the hill to throw him off.

The failure of the apostles at the end of his life is incredible. It is almost beyond imagination. How in the world did
those men who lived with him for three years completely
desert him in his hour of need? Oh, yes, John came back
after fleeing, but we forget that there were some hours
when they were all gone. He was left completely alone
when he was tried, scourged, crowned with thorns, and
condemned to death . . . all alone. Just before the Passion,
Christ had said to them, "I have called you friends for all
that I have heard from my Father I have made known to
you" (Jn 15:15). In a short time these friends would not
stand by him in his troubles. They would leave him, and he
would pray for them, "I have said this to you, that in me
you may have peace" (Jn 16:33). He prayed for them fervently (Jn 17). He predicted they would leave him. "The
hour is coming, has indeed come, when you will be scat-

tered, every man to his home, and will leave me alone; yet I am not alone, for the Father is with me" (Jn 16:32). These men were friends, but their friendship had limitations. He goes on all alone when he needed them the most. There is one fascinating exception to the statement that Jesus was left all alone. That exception is provided by the holy women. The women stayed with him. However, there is a fascinating detail that puts the support of the women in an unusual light. A Jewish woman was not permitted to speak to any man but her father, her husband, her brothers, and very close members of the family. She could not speak to other men. So even the women who followed Jesus probably had very limited conversations with him. We don't quite understand this because we haven't lived in the Orthodox Jewish world. Supra-Orthodox Jews still retain this very rigid segregation of the sexes. It was probably not that rigid at our Lord's time, but we know of the surprise on the part of the Samaritan woman when Christ spoke to her at Jacob's well.

This means that the very few people who could have consoled him could only weep and lament from a distance. They could be there, but they could not directly speak to him, except his mother and his mother's sister Mary, the wife of Clopas. Mary Magdalene probably never had a lengthy conversation with our Lord. The social customs simply did not permit this. There was no way when Christ was suffering that any woman other than his mother and his aunt could possibly have come up and touched him. And so, our Lord was surrounded by loyal followers who could do little to console him. These devoted women are given significant recognition in Scripture, but I don't think they're given enough recognition by the Church today. "There stood by the cross of Jesus his mother, his mother's sister

Mary, the wife of Clopas, Mary Magdalene and the wife of
Zebedee and Salome and many other women who had
come up with him out of Galilee" (Mt 27:55; Mk 15:40; Jn
19:25).

Social custom may explain the strange passage when
Christ is risen from the dead and poor Mary Magdalene,
who is a little bit histrionic, reaches out to the Risen Lord
and he reminds her not to touch him. When I was a student
priest, I used to eat at a restaurant with the unusual name of
"The 42nd Street Glatt". *Glatt* means completely kosher.
The word signified that even the milk served was not taken
from cows on the Sabbath. Once, I ordered a knish. The
waitress could not ask me any questions because she was not
permitted to speak to me. She finally took the menu and
pointed to the two kinds of knishes, buckwheat and blue-
berry. Awareness of this custom gives an insight into
Christ's isolation at his death.

Our Lord was abandoned by his disciples while his faithful followers, almost all women, could offer practically no
comfort because of the social customs. He was there all
alone. His lonely death follows upon the pathetic scene in
the Garden where he is abandoned by his apostles, who fall
asleep when he needs them desperately. One should read
the following passage carefully.

> And they went to a place which was called Gethsemane, and
> he said to his disciples, "Sit here while I pray." And he took
> with him Peter and James and John, and began to be greatly
> distressed and troubled. And he said to them, "My soul is very
> sorrowful, even to death; remain here, and watch." And going
> a little farther, he fell to the ground and prayed that, if it were
> possible, the hour might pass from him. And he said, "Abba,
> Father, all things are possible to you, remove this cup from me;
> yet not what I will, but what you will." And he came and
> found them sleeping, and he said to Peter, "Simon, are you

asleep? Could you not watch one hour? Watch and pray that you may not enter into temptation; the spirit indeed is willing, but the flesh is weak." And again he went away and prayed, saying the same words. And again he came and found them sleeping (Mk 14:32–39).

Part of the Human Condition

Has this happened to you? This is an even more painful question—have you ever fallen asleep on a friend who needed you? That's the haunting question for us all. I know when people have failed me, but I usually can't recognize when I have failed them. Why did Christ go through all this? He did it for you and me so that we will have an example to guide us when we are left alone, one of the most common and painful situations of life. We can know that Jesus Christ has been there before us. His example will give us the wisdom to ask objectively, "Why do friends fail?" Because we are human. Because we have original sin. Because we grow old and weak and are sick and are preoccupied with keeping ourselves together. Why did the apostles fail? Because this was all too much for them. It was beyond their strength. Be prepared for friends to fail you and also for the special grief when someone will say to you, "You failed me."

There are wonderful souls in the world who never failed anyone, and God has blessed them. But even they will die and not be there. It is part of the human condition that we all experience the failure of friends, of loved ones, of spouses, of parents, of children. Some of those who read these lines have suffered the failure of their parents. I think it is the most painful suffering one can go through in this life. I have talked to people who are in their 50s and 60s, and they are still scarred by the things that happened to them a half century ago when their parents failed them. People are hurt by their brothers or sisters, by their spouses, by their children, not only their real children but their surrogate children for whom they have been parent figures.

Better to Love and Lose

Be warned—love and you will get hurt. But it is better for us to love and lose than not to love at all because we are all moving toward an everlasting experience of love. When life does not make sense, the believer must recall that we are moving toward a much more real and everlasting experience of love. Do you realize that you and I are members of an extremely small minority of human beings—the people who are alive just now? Think of the immense number who have died. If you could get back from eternity all the people who once lived in New York City, we could hardly move because of all of them. Think of all those who have ever lived in Europe or in Asia. The vast majority of all human beings are dead. You and I are part of this funny little minority that runs around thinking we're terribly important. What is a more awesome thought is the great number of people who haven't been born yet and who are still coming.

I was walking down a lane in Ireland, and my cousin Father Dohaney said to me, "Do you realize that your relatives walked on this lane for a thousand years?" I could imagine all those generations of folk—Tipperary people—packed into that little village.

Every year, I take our young friars on a marvelous expedition. We go to Ellis Island, the immigration museum in New York Harbor. I found a picture there of Irish people waiting to take a boat 125 years ago. Whenever I look at these strange men with their gaunt beards and the ladies with shawls all wearing rough woolen clothing, I always say to myself, "They are my ancestors, my family." A visit to the immigration museum at Ellis Island is a marvelous spiritual experience. One hundred million Americans, almost half our population, are descended from people who went through Ellis Island or Castle Garden before it. There are innumerable deeply-moving photos of immense numbers of people, and those people are all dead. They have all gone to another world—for everlasting blessedness or a terrible condemnation. Almost all of them suffered from being left alone sometime in their lives. Most of them, one hopes, now live in everlasting peace and joy because they were not afraid to love and lose.

Two Critical Realizations

We don't like to think about the inescapable fact that human life is a quickly passing experience, a river swiftly moving. Part of the answer to the question "What do we do when life doesn't make sense?" is the recognition of that fact. We need to grasp that all things we experience, even the most precious, the love of family and friends, are passing. Any harm or pain that the failure of loved ones brings us is also passing. Life does not simply pass. It goes on into something more beautiful or more terrible, to salvation or to eternal loss. Life's purpose and our attitude toward it must be defined by this conviction if we are believers. We will return to this crucial fact over and over.

The second realization is that Christ has endured and sanctified the pain of the failure of friends by his own life and by his forgiveness of them for their failures. He reproached them, but he did not abandon them. He responded to Peter's protestation of unending loyalty at the Last Supper by saying, "Simon, Simon, behold Satan has demanded to have you, that he might sift you like wheat, but I have prayed for you that your faith may not fail; and when you have turned again, strengthen your brothers . . . . I tell you, Peter, the cock will not crow this day, until you three times deny that you know me" (Lk 22:31–34).

How does one, in practice, put these two ideas together—the passing nature of human experience and the forgiving example of Christ? By the mystics, the answer is called the mystery of the Cross. This mystery is not an abstract intellectual idea or argument but an experienced reality. One can enter into the fullness of this mystery only when one is in fact suffering or has suffered. In this case we are looking at the failure of friends. We see that Christ endures this failure and overcomes this pain in two ways—he forgives Peter ahead of time on the eve of the Passion before the events take place. He then embraces the sorrow but also shows that his Father will bring good out of evil. At the end of the Last Supper and immediately after the prophecy of Peter's denial Jesus said, "You will all fall away because of me this night, for it is written, 'I will strike the shepherd and the sheep of the flock will be scattered.' But after I am raised up, I will go before you into Galilee" (Mt 26:31–32).

Even more powerfully does Jesus assert his confidence that the Father will bring good out of evil in the great prayer that he says in the opening of John 17. "Father, the hour has come; glorify thy Son that the Son may glorify thee, since thou hast given him power over all flesh, to give eternal life to all whom thou hast given him" (1–2).

We have already mentioned Cardinal Newman, a man capable of deep friendship and consequently familiar with suffering. The two go together. The following lines from Newman sum up so well the urgency for using the prism of the mystery of the Cross when you look at life. I quote these lines for your meditation despite Newman's use of an occasional nineteenth-century phrase.

How to Understand Life

Ten thousand things come before us one after another in the course of life, and what do we think about of them? What colour do we give them? Are we to look at all things in a gay and mirthful way? or in a melancholy way? in a desponding or a hopeful way? Are we to make light of life altogether, or to treat the whole subject seriously? Are we to make greatest things of little consequence, or least things of great consequence? Are we to keep in mind what is past and gone, or are we to look to the future, or are we to be absorbed in the present? *How* are we to look at things? [In contemporary language we would say, "What is our attitude toward life?"] This is the question which all persons of observation ask themselves, and answer each in his own way. They wish to think by rule; by something within them, which may harmonise and adjust what is without them. Such is the need felt by reflective minds. Now, let me ask, what *is* the real key, what is the Christian interpretation of this world? What is given us by revelation to estimate and measure this world by? The event of this season,— the Crucifixion of the Son of God.

It is the death of the Eternal Word of God made flesh, which is our great lesson how to think and how to speak of this world. His Cross has put its due value upon every thing which we see, upon all fortunes, all advantages, all ranks, all dignities, all pleasures, upon the lust of the flesh, and the lust of the eyes, and the pride of life. It has set a price on the excitements, the rivalries, the hopes, the fears, the desires, the efforts, the triumphs of mortal man. It has given a meaning to the various, shifting course, the trials, the temptations, the sufferings, of his earthly state. It has brought together and made consistent all that seemed discordant and aimless. It has taught us how to live, how to use this world, what to expect, what to desire, what to hope. It is the tone into which all the strains of this world's music are ultimately to be resolved. . . . The doctrine of the Cross of Christ does but anticipate for us our experience of the world. It is true, it bids us grieve for our sins in the midst of all that smiles and glitters around us; but if we will not heed it, we shall at length be forced to grieve for them from undergoing their fearful punishments. If we will not acknowledge that this world has been made miserable by sin, from the sight of Him on whom our sins were laid, we shall experience it to be miserable by the recoil of those sins upon ourselves.[2]

What Cardinal Newman is saying is: whether you are a believer or an unbeliever, whether you accept the Cross and try to live by it to harmonize the pains, aches, joys, and sorrows of life, or you reject the Cross and turn away from all faith, you will arrive at the same conclusion about the world. This is so because life is an absolutely honest paymaster. At its end life deals out justly the wages we have earned. Those who have lived well, though they may have been very poor and subject to much injustice, will be prepared for the Kingdom of God. And those who have lived badly will encounter the message of the Cross, but this will be for their judgment. Don't doubt it! Rich and poor, just and unjust, criminals and virtuous people, children, the whole crowd, we all, the bad and the good, walk through the same judgment. But for the good, for the innocent, for those who have struggled, for those who have repented, the discordant and painful themes of life will be changed into the music of eternity. "Do not lay up for yourselves treasures on earth, where moth and rust consume and thieves break in

[2] John Henry Newman, *Parochial and Plain Sermons*, VI, Sermon 7 (San Francisco: Ignatius Press, 1987), 1229–30, 1232.

and steal, but lay up for yourselves treasures in heaven" (Mt 6:19–20). Don't doubt for one minute that all will march without exception under the arms of the Cross. There are many who, through no fault of their own, do not know the name of Jesus Christ, or who have not been presented with the Christian message in any way that would have attracted them. There are those who, through no fault of their own, search honestly for God but haven't been given the abundant grace that you and I have received. Our Lord says of them, "I have other sheep that are not of this fold; I must bring them also, and they will heed my voice. So there shall be one flock and one shepherd" (Jn 10:16).

During the time I was working on this book, we were all deeply moved by the frightful sufferings of Moslems and Christians in Bosnia and the incredible sufferings of the people in Rwanda. Some of these people were non-Christians, but I am sure that our Crucified Savior was there among them, and that their sufferings, their needs, their search for God will not be lost for eternity. I pray for them that they will be saved. Many are Christians of simple faith. They are blessed to unite themselves consciously in this suffering with Christ.

But on the other side there are those who take upon themselves almost mindlessly the terrible role of being the enemies of the mystery of the Cross. They appear on your television every day. They come into your living room to mock the teachings of Jesus Christ and to belittle his Church. I pray for them because they are in far greater danger than the people in Bosnia or Rwanda. They are in eternal danger. For myself, I am as St. Paul was, "in fear and trembling" (1 Cor 2:3). Our Lord teaches that from those to whom much is given, much will be expected. I look at my life, and I see the times I have failed miserably. I have failed my friends. I have failed my family. I have failed many times. And so when others fail me I try to say, "Well, this is some penance for my own failures."

Cardinal Newman ends his essay with these startling words: "They alone are able truly to enjoy this world, who begin with the world unseen. They alone enjoy it, who have first abstained from it. . . . They alone inherit it, who take it as a shadow of the world to come, and who for that world to come relinquish it." [3]

The Changeless Friend

We have all experienced the failure of friends. For one reason or another they were not there when we needed them. We know that no matter what happens, if we turn to him, there is one Friend who never fails, who is always there. Our faith constantly brings us to that Changeless Friend. Prayer is essential here because it is the only way for us to encounter our Friend. He is changeless because he no longer walks in this world of change. Through him we come into contact with that multitude of friends who have gone before us to that bright world where he waits for us— his Father's house. Even if you have to pray in pain or agony as he did in the Garden, you will soon enough find him there in the shadows. Prayer, deep personal prayer coming from the heart of our being, is the way that we can embrace and be embraced by our Changeless Friend.

[3] Ibid., 1235.

— *Prayer* —

O LORD JESUS CHRIST, thank you for leaving me the example of your sorrow and aloneness in the Garden of Olives. Without that example, it would be so much more difficult for me to go on when no one is there for me. I am grateful for all those whom you have given me along the way as loving friends and also for the charge you have given me to be a friend to others. But sooner or later we must all go on alone—and there is always that place in my heart where no one can come but you. Without your presence, that inner solitude becomes oppressive, even devastating—a wasteland of howling winds and dark nights. But when you are there with me—and only you can come there—my whole life is filled with light and I can go on even in the midst of great trials.

Be with me, Lord, in the dark time, and let me rise from the darkness because you are there. Be that friend who brings to me all that I may have lost—the love of mother and father, of sister and brother, of friend and teacher. When the final hours of this journey come and I must leave all behind, walk with me down the corridor that has neither steps nor time. Protect me from the enemies of my soul and from the snarling voice of the accuser. Give me your hand and I shall be saved.

For the rest, let me be a loyal friend to many as they struggle in life, and let me be just and forgiving to my enemies. Let me not expect more of friends than they can give—but let me give them more than they expect. Let me not expect too much of others who, like myself, struggle under the burden of life, but rather let me be, as best I can, a friend who does not fail. May we be friends in you, the Changeless Friend of us all.

3

When Our Security Is Threatened

What do we do when life doesn't make sense because our economic or personal security is threatened or even taken away? We are well aware that in this life our Lord Jesus Christ had little or no security. Certainly from the beginning he had no personal security as we understand it. "After the Wise Men had left, the angel of the Lord appeared in a dream to Joseph and said, 'Get up, and take the child and his mother and go as fast as you can into Egypt, and stay there. For Herod will soon be looking for the child to kill him' " (Mt 2:13).

The life of Christ began with danger, and insecurity followed him every step of the way. Economic uncertainty was his constant companion. Furthermore he did nothing to encourage people who had possessions to feel secure in this world. In fact, if anything, he actively discouraged feelings of security. For example, in the parable of the rich farmer he speaks of a man who is called to the Last Judgment just after building fine new barns. The man said to himself, "I don't have to worry, I can enjoy everything. My life is at last secure." And he heard the words, "This night your soul is required of you" (Lk 12:20). This parable, like many others, does nothing to enhance a sense of security based on wealth. The message of Christ's parables and his life is this: if you are trying to make some sense out of life, it is important to decide that worldly or material security is an illusion. Decide today that if you are seeking security and a perfectly safe situation in this life, you are pursuing something that is in itself very insecure—even unreal.

A False Sense of Security

Insecurity and uncertainty are facts of life. Obviously, people have a right to some economic security from what they can earn by work and careful spending. However, this right is more properly seen as our obligation to take care of ourselves so as not to be a burden to others. What has happened in the rich nations is that security has become a false god. When I studied psychology twenty-five years ago, personnel directors commented that graduates fresh out of college were looking for jobs and inquiring about the retirement policy. Above all else they had a need to be secure. That feeling of security turned out to be a fraud. It caused people to forget that our worldly accomplishments are certainly passing and temporary. Nothing could be more obvious than the fact that we are not permanently here. If you feel secure in this world, you feel secure unwisely and are clinging to a shadow. Our economic superiority over some other nations causes us to have these false feelings of security. Recently government pension programs and Social Security have been in deep financial trouble. They are said to be short about a trillion dollars. Everyone relied on these funds. The same is true of health insurance. The names health and life insurance are part of the great deception about security. It is really sickness and death insurance. They are collected only when you are sick or you die. Job security used to be the great prize in the United States. I spoke to a man recently who was delivering a package for the poor. He said to me, "I worked for twenty-nine years for a big corporation, and now I'm looking for a job. I never thought I would look for a job in my whole life."

Another painful fact is that the United States is becoming a relatively poor country. This is very clear when you travel overseas. As an itinerant preacher I found that out very quickly. I can remember the days when, if you went to another country with American dollars you could have your lunch for a dollar and still leave a nice tip. American money had incredible purchasing power. When I was in London recently, I became very well aware that American money doesn't amount to much anymore. For three days in a row I had my lunch at an American-style fast-food place. I had the same lunch every day, a rubbery chicken sandwich and a cup of tea, for twice what it would cost in New York.

I had to go through the Narita Airport in Tokyo in 1991, but I was prepared ahead of time. I had a five-hour layover including noontime, so I brought with me a lunch and a can of soda. I sat there writing sermons, munching on my tuna-salad sandwich, and staring at a sign advertising a little styrofoam cup of coffee priced seven times the cost in the United States. I could not even afford to starve in Japan.

With the exception of the few remaining people who remember the Depression, Americans are for the most part unprepared to think about economic insecurity. This unpreparedness and fear might in the long run turn some people to God. Robert Bellah, who often brings Christian values into his analysis of American life, noted:

> Whatever white collar America once assumed about getting ahead, trusting employers, or simply staying employed, the reality of the 1990's is becoming clear: The deal is off. [Formerly] there was an implied contract, "You give us your loyalty and we'll give you security." [Now] as corporate America shrinks, consolidates and otherwise cuts costs, it is

squeezing more people out of work—and more work out of people—than ever before.[1]

If you happen to be reading these lines after the recession of the 1990s is over, perhaps in boom or bust times like the late 1980s, keep in mind that what is true in physics is true in economics: "What goes up, comes down."

Even if a person were to have a great deal of apparent economic security, what about health? What about the peculiar vicissitudes of life? What about the hundreds of possible calamities that could come in an instant to cause one to lose one's security? Loss of employment, loss of one's own home, danger to health, aging, and, in the later years of life, chronic illness—these are all things that reveal the lie underlying a false sense of earthly security. What is the answer?

A Sense of Peace When Insecure

The obvious answer is Christ's teaching not to put your trust in possessions. It is not wrong to feel a little more comfortable when we are more secure than we were. That's fine. I suppose the Christ Child may have felt a little more safe and sound when Joseph and Mary got back to their home in Nazareth after Herod was dead. It is by no means wrong to enjoy a bit of security and peace of mind, but don't put your ultimate trust in anything that passes away. Don't be surprised when your earthly security is threatened, because it is really always tenuous, but we simply don't realize it. Since security in this world is called into question every day, by illness, mishap, and accident, what then should we do? We

---

[1] Robert N. Bellah, "Small Face-to-Face Christian Communities in a Mean-Spirited & Polarized Society", *New Oxford Review*, 60 (June 1992): 17–18.

need to follow the example of Christ and trust in God alone. This will permit us to have peace and trust in God even when we experience insecurity, because we already know that any sense of security in this world is an illusion.

What Trust in God Really Means

Trust in God does not mean that everything is going to work out just the way we want it to, that everything is going to be peaches and cream. Trust in God doesn't mean that he is going to restore the false sense of security that we had before. It means that, whatever happens, we believe that God is there with us and that, if we cling to him, he will bring good out of evil, even out of the evil that he has only permitted to happen. I must make up my mind now that in the darkest hour of life, I will believe that God is with me. And I believe that he will be with you and all who turn to him and even with those who do not know enough to turn to him. This life at its best or worst passes quickly, but God is always there. In the end, the good and the bad walk over the very narrow threshold of physical death. They pass beyond the veil of physical appearances and are standing in the presence of God, where each must render an account and rely on God's mercy.

Think about all this for a minute. An elderly person is very sick, terminally ill. I recall my good friend Sister Cuthbert of the Sisters of the Sacred Heart of Mary in Tarrytown, New York. She had worked as a secretary and receptionist in the archdiocesan offices until she was ill, well into her late seventies. Now she was on the edge of death. As I was leaving at the end of what we both knew was to be my last visit, she saw my tears and said, "Don't be upset,

Father, I know that our Lady will come to get me soon and bring me home." What a beautiful expression, what marvelous hope! She knew with great certainty that she would pass from this place of pain through the short corridor of death into the hands of God. She had been a sister devoted to our Lady for half a century—of course the Mother of Christ would go with her. I feel confident of her salvation. She was the kind of person who worked at being a faithful friend of God and a follower of Christ, and Christ doesn't forget his friends.

Think of a martyr, of someone facing death by torture. I recall a cold shudder coming over me as I walked through the busy downtown section of Kyoto, Japan. The guidebook mentioned that at this very crossroads the martyrs of Nagasaki (who were Catholic converts from Kyoto) had been condemned to death by a shogun. Although the Church had functioned openly in Japan for a while, the shoguns had turned against it. Twenty-six people, including priests, religious, and laity, were condemned to death by torture. Their ears were sliced off, and in the dead of winter they were put on a forced march for almost a month, going from town to town in Japan to frighten others away from joining the new religion. They knew what fate awaited them at the end of their journey—death by crucifixion. Their freezing march came to an end when they were crucified overlooking Nagasaki on February 5, 1597. These martyrs all remained steadfast throughout that interminable torture. With their dying breath, hanging on the cross, they shouted to one another, encouraging each other with words of faith and trust in God. They did not expect to be delivered from physical death. They did not expect the sky to open and an angel to come down and remove them from the cross. No, they expected to pass from this world into eternal life. Whatever prayers they may have offered for some mitigation of their punishments had apparently not been granted, but they died with a tremendous faith and provided the Japanese people with a marvelous example of martyrdom and courage. Whether it is the ancient martyrs being fed to the wild beasts, a terrifying and horrible death, or someone killed in our own time in a concentration camp, the martyrs pass through the thin wall of death into a reality where there is no change, no pain and sorrow, no time at all as we know it. Without the pain and glory of martyrdom we will follow the same route and pass through the same door of death. Perhaps we must go through Purgatory (which the saints tell us not to fear, because there we are in the safe hands of God) to prepare our souls to be totally open to the salvation of Christ and the glorious reality of eternal life. This is a reality that even our Lord could not describe to us because it goes beyond our power of human thought.

The Real Fear

There is also the other side that we have to think of. I seldom write on this topic because it is so painful. What happens to the wicked? For some reason, in recent years, we have pretended that no one is really wicked. Everyone is supposed to be really nice, and we all share in this pretense. No, there are wicked people around. Some are obvious, like willful and unrepentant murderers. But think of those who have deprived millions of people of their savings through chicanery and larceny involving the savings and loan industry. The Bible tells us that to deprive ordinary people or the poor people of their wages is a sin that cries to heaven for vengeance (Dt 24:14–15).

A good woman recently spoke to me with tears in her eyes. "I worked for twenty-five years for such and such a corporation, and they declared bankruptcy, and then they were gobbled up, and all the faithful employees were left high and dry. . . . Yeah, they declared bankruptcy, but some big people made out very nicely while most others were left out on the sidewalk." This kind of thing cries out to God for vengeance even though at times it may be a legal maneuver that covers a terrible crime. In fact, instead of being angry at those who do these things, one might feel sorry for them, for they will answer for this on the Day of Judgment.

The Scriptures give advice to us on our attitude toward those who profit unjustly. These are the words of Psalm 37, which I have translated freely:

> Don't get excited because of the wicked. Don't be envious of those who do wrong, for they will soon fade away like the grass and wither like weeds. Trust in the Lord and do good, and so you will live in the land and enjoy security. Delight in the Lord, and he will fulfill the desires of your heart. Put yourself in the hands of the Lord, trust in him, and he will act. He will give you justice in the light, and your rights will shine like the sun at noon. Be silent before the Lord, and wait patiently for him. Don't upset yourself over those who prosper on their way, over those who carry out evil plans. Don't get angry and give up rage. For the wicked shall be destroyed but those who wait for the Lord shall possess the earth. A little while and the wicked shall be no more. Though you look for him carefully in his home, he will not be there. The meek shall possess the earth and be delighted in abundant prosperity. . . . The Lord knows the ways of the blameless, and their inheritance will last forever. They will not be ashamed in evil times. In the day of famine they will be fed abundantly, but the wicked shall perish.

This is an extremely important teaching we seem to have forgotten. Somehow or other, modern people have forgotten that God promises to balance the scales in the end, but only after this passing life is over. Let me put it this way: if an angel of the Lord appeared to you, and you have been a victim of social and financial injustice, and he said, "Would you like your rights now, or would you like your rights in eternity?" for heaven's sake, don't say you want them now, or someone else will come along and steal them next week. Why would you want them now in this valley of tears? Eternity lasts forever. That is what we learn from the life of Christ, of our Lady, and of the apostles. Our Lord Jesus Christ trusted in God. His enemies tormented him on the Cross. "He saved others; he cannot save himself. He is the King of Israel; let him come down from the cross, and we will believe in him" (Mt 27:42).

Jesus trusted in his Father to save him. He died and was laid in the tomb. His Divinity did not need the Resurrection. We needed the Resurrection. We needed the glorious Resurrection of our Lord Jesus Christ so that we would know that the wicked do not succeed, so that we would know enough not to place our trust in the powers of this world. We who are followers of Christ should not trust in the security of this world, because we would be building our castles of sand. Jesus Christ as an infant, as a child and an adult, had people plotting against his life. You might say that he spent his whole life as a fugitive and almost never knew the kind of security that most of us enjoy. But he was given victory over all evil.

Real Security in the Real World

We need to believe that on the other side of this very thin material wall, the world we perceive with our senses, there is a world without time or ambiguity. It is a world no longer in the process of dying. In this world we are temporarily in a place of incompleteness, of adventure, of partial illusion. Though incomprehensible, the possibilities of the next world are very clear. There is either an eternal life or an eternal loss. I don't know about you, but I do not wish to perish forever. I suspect that you, like myself, want to see your dear ones in the eternal life of the next world. I am sure that, like everyone else, you do not want the good things that you have cherished in this life to disappear forever. The message of the glorious Resurrection of Jesus Christ is that what we have loved will not disappear, that the good things will last forever. That hope is the meaning of trust in God. Many Christians in the course of the centuries, including many members of the clergy and religious orders, have trusted in this world and at the same time have tried to trust in eternity. They've had a foot in both camps. It's a mistake. Cardinal Wolsey, who had served King Henry VIII so faithfully, as he was dying in Henry's disfavor, is supposed to have said, "Had I served my God as well as I have served my king, he would not have left me in my old age, naked to my enemies." Yes, he, like all too many others, tried to have a stake in both worlds.

But you must know that there are ordinary people who are very clear about where they have placed their security. Some time ago I was going through a huge pile of mail and came across this letter. It's an astonishing letter. There's a punch line at the end that blew me away when I read it. I called the lady and asked her if I could use the letter. She gave me permission to quote her letter verbatim. She said:

> I am very happy to hear you speak about life and what it means. It is a shame that the world doesn't see it, no matter how young or old. You see, I too believe in life very strongly. We had two sons with a totally paralyzing disease. We lost one

some six years ago, when he was 24 years old, just one month before his 25th birthday. Our other son is going to be 29 this August. Thanks be to God, no matter what happens. It is my understanding that the doctors asked if we wanted to treat them or let them die. They call themselves experts. Without nutrition or hydration, they would have simply died. You see, my son is on a feeding machine. He has two tubes into his stomach, one is feeding and the other is the drainage tube. Also, he's on twelve different kinds of medication, and so often he needs blood. He is bed-ridden. You see, he's all but a vegetable. But there is still life, no matter what. It's not up to us to take a life. When the Lord wants him, he will say that it is time for him to come home. I know that you are not supposed to get angry, and that it's a sin, but I know that I can't help myself when I hear that they want to do away with life, and not feed people through a feeding tube. They say it's because they want to give them some dignity. That's a bunch of bull. That's because they don't have to take care of them, and they worry more about the almighty buck than they do about life itself. Why can't they see beauty in the way our Lord Jesus did when he was walking among us? How Jesus cared and loved us. Jesus said, "Judge not, unless you shall be held in judgment." How can I judge, knowing that they are wrong about life? You see, I take care of my son at home and also my mother. I go on because, you see, I know in my heart and soul that Jesus is always with me, no matter what. And Jesus gave me his strength to do what I must do. My husband is still working in another state. *And even though the two boys were not my own sons, but stepchildren*, I still felt as if they were my own. I have been taking care of this boy for ten years and, with the Lord's help, always will. Even though it has been hard work I will not put my son or my mother in a nursing home.

This is an astonishing letter, isn't it? These invalid boys are not her sons. This woman knows what's important, and she has a very real sense of security. Hers is not security in this world, rather security in the world to come, real security. I'm not trying to sell insecurity, but I'm trying to point out that there is a false security in this world, a security that fades away, no matter how rich, how powerful, how young, how gifted, how wealthy a person may be. "This night they require your soul of you." And that word can be heard by anyone, at any time.

In New York we live in a city of incredible extremes, an apocalyptic place. I only stay here because I think it is where God wants me to be, and after sixty years I have learned to live with its madness and its astonishing mystical invitations. On Christmas evening I always spend that special time with men who have nothing but what they carry in a little plastic bag. All they have is our Padre Pio Shelter. They are very insecure. Yet they are fairly peaceful and quite capable of having a great Christmas party. At the same time, we have in this city people worth millions of dollars who are often sad and closed-in on themselves. They may be totally miserable, surrounded by comforts but not by happiness.

The late Joseph Fitzpatrick, S.J., was a world-famous sociologist, a model priest, and a quintessential New Yorker. The only boast he ever made was that at one time he was voted "Puerto Rican of the Year" because of his life work with the Hispanic community. He told the friars of an interesting event in the life of the great labor negotiator Father Benjamin L. Massey, S.J.

In the most crucial days of the labor movement, Father Massey was often called out to negotiate strikes. He was out in the coal mines when John L. Lewis and the United Mine Workers were facing the mine owners. Lewis himself was there with his craggy face and his big head of white hair, looking almost like a prophet. On the left were the mine workers, and on the right were the mine owners, all very wealthy men. And in the middle were Father Massey and a couple of other clergymen who were trying to negotiate. John L. Lewis got up and said, looking at the mine workers first, "Friends," then he looked at the clergy and said, "Romans," and finally he looked at the mine owners and said, "Millionaires".

Friends, Romans, and Millionaires. In New York we have many millionaires. Some are very generous. New York has many hospitals, public facilities, museums, and services that wealthy people substantially donated and support. As a matter of fact there is one church in New York that they call the "Fire Escape". They say that the fellow who built it was trying to get out of hell when he donated the church.

I can testify myself that there are many people who are very well off who help our work with the poor with no fanfare or payback other than the prayers of friars, the sisters, and the poor. The friars were trying to make an old, dilapidated school building into a social and religious education center in a very poor section of the Bronx. I was showing this project to a very successful attorney and mentioned that I was going to try to make the old auditorium into a gym. He asked, "How much do you think it will cost to do that?" I explained that I had to put in bathrooms and backstops with other equipment, so I estimated about $50,000. He said, "Wait a minute", and then wrote a check for that amount. Of course, he had to call an ambulance because I had to be taken to the hospital in a state of shock.

Another very fine lady didn't even know we were having to struggle to furnish the center when she wrote me about her daughter. I had never heard of this lady but wrote her a little note on a bumpy airplane where I usually do my correspondence. I assured her of our prayers. She wrote back, "My husband and I are celebrating our 45th wedding anni-

versary, so here's a check for $45,000." These are examples
of people who are well off and relatively secure but also
generous. They should be and they are. We are delighted to
help them and the poor at the same time. It's a help all
around.

Whether you work in the stock market or the stock
yards, remember you're not secure. We're all living on the
edge, and we're all approaching eternity at exactly the same
rate of speed: 24 hours a day, seven days a week. Here are
some suggestions on how to keep your need for security in
line with the Gospel.

Some Suggestions

First of all, get your priorities in order. I know that most
readers are sensibly concerned about their economic security. Others are concerned about their physical health. The
important thing is to put your treasure where it ought to be.
Repeat to yourselves the words of Christ, "Lay up for yourselves treasures in heaven, where neither moth nor rust con-
sumes and thieves do not break in and steal" (Mt 6:20). We
owe it to ourselves, and we need to give an example to our
families and friends, many of whom have become incredibly
materialistic. We need to remind them by frugality in our
use of things, by modesty in what we wear, and by the
plainness of things we use. If you are a Christian, you need
to live as one who, convinced that here we have no lasting
city, is seeking the Kingdom of God.

Second, we need to overcome our feelings of financial
insecurity by generosity. It is necessary to be generous when
you are secure and even when your security is threatened. If
you have a little to give, give it joyously. Remember the

poor widow whom Christ praised because she gave all that she had into the temple treasury.

Third, we need to give an example of generosity. An old priest who is not well does his Christmas shopping in a few minutes and at the same time gives a great example to all his family. He sends me labels for all his relatives and friends and gives me money to buy meals for poor people in the name of each one of them. All the relatives get a letter saying that Father Ed arranged to pay for a meal for a poor person in their name on Christmas Day. These notes bring with them not only the prayers of the poor and of our community but also a good example. Cardinal Cooke used to say, "The best gift one friend can give to another is prayer." Just think of all the junk, expensive toys (I don't mean children's toys, I mean adult toys), the garbage that is bought at Christmas time and given to people who don't need these things or want them or know what to do with them. We do want to give a little something that's attractive—maybe something that is a little unusual. That's laudable. But if you see the prices on things advertised in the paper for "the people who have everything", you realize that they don't have everything; they don't have a prayer. Some of the people who have everything have nobody praying for them, and they could use a few prayers.

"Do not lay up for yourselves treasures on earth, where moth and rust consume and thieves break in and steal, but lay up for yourselves treasures in heaven . . ." (Mt 6:19-20). These are words not of St. Paul, not of St. John, not of St. Peter. These are the words of Jesus Christ. They are powerful and awesome words. Those who have followed these words will have a security that no one can take from them. They will know where they are and where they are going while the world does not know where it is or where it is going. We are standing right next to an invisible wall. And on the other side of that wall is an eternal reality. The mystical poet William Blake aptly observed that in the other world there is a gate. On one side of that gate is the Portal of Heaven. On the other side is the Hell Gate. The reality of God neither changes nor can be changed; it is a reality incredibly and unspeakably beautiful in its reward for those who follow God; a reality unspeakably terrible and horrible for those who do not. Modern people are worried about their security. Well they *may* worry, because their world is quickly slipping into paganism, and the blindness it brings is about the true meaning of life.

What We Should Worry About

We need to be insecure about the right things. I am very insecure about the fact that I have not spoken up enough against evil. I'm insecure at times that I have gone along with evil in a passive sort of way. I know that on Judgment Day I will be asked about these things. But I am not insecure about the things of this world. It is harder for a lay person than for me. I'm a friar. One day I had a hole in my sock, so someone gave me a few dollars to buy a pair of socks. Our little community is trying to take St. Francis seriously. We don't save up. We don't have any real estate. And yet we are secure. We are not worried. The Lord will provide. If at any moment we friars decided we'd better start investing money and saving our funds, then I would be frightened; but I am not frightened now, because we have relied on the Lord.

In your life, especially as a lay person, or as a diocesan priest, or as a member of a religious community that runs an institution, you cannot rely on the Lord in the same way. But you personally must rely on him. If you trust in the funds of this world, if you trust in worldly possessions, you will be deceived. You will be ripped off. Even if you have lots of worldly possessions when you die, you will be cheated by all of them. Your own possessions will cheat you. They are the biggest cheat of all. They are fools' gold. Rich or poor, a good Christian is generous and is most of all reliant on God. St. Paul, who had nothing when he traveled around the world, earning his daily bread as a tentmaker, preaching and asking for little, wrote, "I am sure that neither death, nor life, nor angels, nor principalities, nor powers, nor things present, nor things to come, nor height, nor depth, nor anything else in all creation, can separate us from the love of God in Christ Jesus, our Lord" (Rom 8:38-39). And that—and nothing else—is security.

— *Prayer* —

O GOD, OUR FATHER, you give us each day our daily bread. You give us what we need and often much more than what we need. You tell us in the words of your Divine Son to trust in you and to rely on you for all things. Often we are filled with fear. We are afraid to lose our security, our place in life, our health, our reputation, what we style as our importance. We are afraid to live and more afraid to die. Give us your Holy Spirit that we may find our peace in you. Strengthen us in hours of need. Most of all, may your Holy Spirit teach us to see what is truly important and to surrender that which is really unimportant and perhaps an obstacle on our road to you. May our Lord Jesus Christ, the poor carpenter of Nazareth, the homeless preacher of the roads, the man condemned to death and deprived of all earthly things, including this life, be our model. May we not wish to be more secure than he was. And when things are taken from us and our security fails, may his example and life be a guiding light to us through the short journey of this life. Heavenly Father, you alone have riches to give that time cannot carry away. You alone can give us that Kingdom which does not perish. We pray, O Lord, that through the example of your Son and the grace of your Holy Spirit, we and all of those dear to us may have a true security based on the acceptance of your Divine Will. May we have eyes to see beyond this world and hearts to cherish that which does not pass away, but which lasts forever. Amen.

4

When the Church Lets Us Down

Scarcely a week goes by that people do not tell me that the Church or some representative of the Church has failed them and even hurt them badly. Sometimes these wounded Christians are sad, but more frequently they are very angry. Occasionally they forget that neither I nor any other priest nor any bishop represents the entire Church. It is painful for them and painful for us. To tell the truth, probably the closer one is to the Church the more one is likely to be hurt by the Church. I suspect that the person in the world who is most often hurt by the Church is the Pope himself, for he is constantly under criticism from all sides—not only from the attacks of those outside the Church, but also from the disgruntled complaints of those within it. The question arises for all of us from Pope to parishioner, "How can the Church fail us so often and still be the Mystical Body of Christ?" Surely we are justified in expecting better care of us from the historical representative of the loving Savior of the world.

Part of our problem is that we use this expression "the Church" to describe a number of things that are related but are to some degree quite different from one another. Obviously the word *church* means different things. It can simply mean a building. It can mean a particular denomination, like the Congregational Church. It can mean a parish or a diocese. "I got in trouble with the local church." It can mean everybody in the world who is a Christian, or it can mean everyone in the world who is a Catholic, a member of the "Catholic Church". The word *catholic* means "universal", from the Greek words *kata holos*, that is, "from out of the whole universe".

Another source of confusion when we speak of the Catholic Church is how membership is defined. When we speak about the Catholics of the United States, we are constantly told in the newspaper that 54 percent of Catholics, to cite a commonly given figure, don't agree with the bishops on this or that. Who is this 54 percent? They are a percentage of what? The pollsters simply ask people, "Are you a Catholic?" Once, when I was chaplain of Children's Village, I taught a boy who said he was a Catholic, and we prepared him for baptism and First Communion. Then we found out that he was a "Catholic" because his cousin played basketball at the CYO center in Harlem. It was the only affiliation the family had, so they thought they were Catholics. The college students hired by the poll-takers call on the phone and say, "Are you a Catholic?" If you say "Yes", they ask, "Do you agree with the Pope on birth control?" Some say "No." So these dissidents become part of the percentage that disagrees with the Pope. We have no idea if these are Catholics who support the Church, or ever even attend a church.

A young lady in my family going to a Catholic school was taught not only that God was a woman but that Jesus was a woman. Her teachers need therapy, long-term therapy. What does it mean even when someone says, "I'm a member of the Catholic Church"? What does it mean when Phil Donahue or some other raconteur says, "I'm a Catholic", or when Madonna or some blasphemous entertainer says, "I'm a Catholic"? They are exploiting the Catholic Church and are making use of the more active membership that they

once had in it. By their endeavors, they are certainly attack-
ing the Church and blaspheming both the Church and her
Founder. What, then, does "the Church" mean?

What Does "Church" Mean?

First of all, it means the Mystical Body of Christ spoken of
so powerfully by St. Paul. "For no man ever hates his own
flesh but nourishes it and cherishes it, as Christ does the
Church, for we are members of his body" (Eph 5:29–30).
"He is the head of the body, the church" (Col 1:18). There
is a spiritual reality that stands behind the visible Church,
the Body of Christ united in a profoundly spiritual way
with all of his members. The lifeblood of this Mystical Body
is the grace of God. Yet the Church herself teaches that you
cannot restrict membership in the Church to those who are
in the state of grace. This was defined at the time of the
Reformation. Some of the reformers said that only those
who were in the state of grace were members of the
Church. The bishops of the Catholic Church rejected this
idea of a church of saints. Those in sin are not getting any
benefit from being members of the Church, but still they
are members. They are sick members. They are members in
trouble. One does not get excommunicated from the
Church if one simply falls from the state of grace.

Most of the time, when we say "the Church", we mean
the visible, external Church led by the bishops and the pope
and also all the other people who have responsibility, the
clergy, religious, the active laity, the parish council, the St.
Vincent de Paul Society, and so forth. Someone says, "I
work for the Church." "Who do you work for?" They say,
"St. Mary's Hospital". That's "the Church". "I work for the

Church and they're cheap." Does it mean the chancery or diocesan office, or is it their parish? These are a whole series of questions that you want to keep in mind when people say that "the Church" failed them. Usually, when people say that the Church failed them, they mean their parish, or the diocese, or even the diocesan bishop. They may also mean the Church in the United States, or—that most unacceptable expression—"the American Church". (I don't know about you, but I do not belong to "the American Church". I belong to the Catholic Church in the United States. Who's the head of this "American" Church?)

Indeed, you might find an "American Catholic Church", because silly people start independent little churches on their own. There used to be a storefront church in Harlem called St. Mary's Mystical Rose Independent Catholic Church. This was the operation of an enterprising clergyman who decided he'd go Catholic but keep his hands directly on things and not get involved with the Swiss Guard and all of that. Every once in a while somebody drops out and starts an "Orthodox Catholic Church", or the "Old Catholic Church". If someone told me that in five years we would have a schism in the Catholic Church in the United States and that it would be called the American Catholic Church, I wouldn't be the slightest bit surprised. Some people seem to be heading that way already. And it will eventually all come to nothing.

Whatever the meaning, almost everyone reading this book can say, "The Church has failed me." It could be the parish, the diocese, the Catholic school, an institution within the Church, a Catholic publication, or the bishops. Everyone can make that claim. Almost every priest or religious can say the same thing and has some legitimate complaint or peeve about something that has happened in his long life of service to the Church—some place where he was dropped out or overlooked or cashiered or not understood. I've been a religious for forty-five years, and I can tell you that often I've been angry at a particular segment of the Church. The possibilities of being hurt are enormous, and they are greater the more one is involved. For example, generous people come to the Church looking for an opportunity to serve, to give substantially of their time and energy. Maybe they give their whole lives in religious vocations. For years things go well, and they are appreciated or at least given the opportunity to work hard and get something done. And then there is a changing of the guard. New leaders come in, and those of the "old guard" are in the way. Little regard is given to all they have done with little or no personal recognition. The feeling comes over them that God himself has no regard for what they have done. They become, understandably but unwisely, angry at God, or at the whole Church from the pope down. It's a terrible feeling. I know. The same thing may happen on a lesser scale to those who are loyal parishioners and members of the Church. They have been generous to the point of sacrifice. They have given till it hurts—and then a new pastor or a new administrator comes, and they are completely forgotten. They know that God did not do this, but emotionally they feel that they have been rejected. One hears echoes of such feelings in the words of the prophets against the Hebrews, in the writings of Paul and John.

Perhaps the worst of all these experiences is to have one's loved ones led astray and taught error by those who represent the Church. I have heard this bitter complaint from parents who sacrificed to give their children a religious education only to discover that it was either grossly deficient or even patently contradictory to the teachings of the Gospel and the Church. Insult is added to injury when there seems to be an inadequate response to legitimate complaints on the part of the ecclesiastical authorities. Admittedly, authorities are often limited in what they can do, far more limited than people assume. But still, the feeling is that the Church has let us down.

Why the Church Fails

When we are thinking clearly, we see that if Church leaders fail us it is not the Mystical Body of Christ. It is not our Divine Savior who fails us. Keep this in mind, because otherwise you will get angry at God. "I'm not going to Church anymore. God let me down." God didn't let you down. Msgr. Stoopnagle, or Sister Mary Officious, or Brother Grinch let you down. That's who let you down. They let God down, too.

The reason the Church fails us is that it is made up of human beings. The Church is a collection of people with original sin. I'm not talking about the heavenly Church of the saints or even that part of the life of the Church where the sacraments remain untouched in their integrity because that's the way Christ instituted them. (If you receive a sacrament from a priest who is unworthy, you still receive the sacrament.) I'm not referring to the Church that gives us the Bible, the Church that certified the Old Testament and identified the books of the New Testament. I'm not referring to the apostolic teaching of the Church, given by Christ and handed on under the guidance of the Holy Spirit.

It is the human side of the Church that can hurt everyone, and yet this human side also does an inestimable amount of good. At the same time, the human side can break your heart. I have worked for the Church all my life. A few years ago I celebrated my fiftieth anniversary as an altar boy. I got hurt when I was an altar boy: I was corrected when I didn't deserve it. I went to Catholic schools for about twenty-five years, and I was hurt by some of my teachers. But I was helped by many more than those who hurt me. The same thing is true of priests and bishops I have known. I have been hurt by a few and helped by many. I've been hurt by religious communities but greatly helped by them. The problem is that when these representatives of the Church hurt me, I had the same angry reaction as a person who feels that God has failed him. It happens to us all.

Let me give you some examples of people in modern times who have been badly hurt by the Church. You'll be very surprised. Padre Pio, the marvelous stigmatic priest, was basically held in house arrest for decades at the order of the Holy See. From the time he received the stigmata till his death, Padre Pio never left the little town where he lived in San Giovanni Rotundo. Never. For years he was not even permitted to offer Mass in public.

The Capuchin priest Solanus Casey, who is presently proposed for beatification, never heard a confession in his life. Only once or twice did he ever preach a real sermon. That was because the authorities in the order thought that he was not bright enough. For the same reason he was never able to vote in the elections of the order. Probably the greatest Capuchin who ever lived in the United States, he was not permitted to preach or hear confessions. I must say that he never looked angry about this terrible indignity, which was totally undeserved. Perhaps that's why he may be declared a saint.

Going back into Church history we find out that St. Alphonsus Ligouri, now honored as a Doctor of the Church, had to withdraw from the order he founded, the Redemptorists, so that they would not be suppressed. And he himself was not permitted to offer Mass in the Papal States, although he was a bishop—incredible! St. Joan of Arc was burned at the stake by sentence of the bishop of Beauvais and eleven theologians. In the prison tower in Rouen, you can see on one side the decree of condemnation leading to the execution of Joan of Arc; and on the other side of the tower, the papal decree, twenty years later, exonerating her and condemning her judges. Even though she had appealed to the pope, the bishop did not honor this appeal, and he himself incurred an ecclesiastical censure.

Don't be surprised that even popes get hurt by the Church. A friend of his told me that Pope Paul VI welcomed death. His years as pope were incredibly difficult, a time of immense turmoil in the Church. A bishop who preached one of the Masses at St. Peter's for the repose of the soul of Paul VI at the time of his death said in his sermon, "Paul, we did not love you."

An Incredible Story

Let me tell you an incredible story of a bishop who was terribly hurt by the Church for thirty years. He was a bishop who lived in New York, Bonaventure Brodrick. He worked as vicar of religious of the New York Archdiocese from 1940 to 1943. Bishop Brodrick earned his living most of his life by running a gasoline station upstate. Until we had these super new gas stations, there used to be a funny little gadget on the end of the pump nozzle that caused it to stop automatically when the tank was full. That gadget was invented and patented by Bishop Bonaventure Brodrick. He lived partially on the income from it.

I have been able to reconstruct this incredible story, which goes back to after the Spanish American War when the United States took over Cuba. For some reason it was decided to make an American priest, Father Brodrick, auxiliary bishop of Havana. Bishop Brodrick went down to Cuba, and shortly after that the Cubans decided they didn't want an American bishop. He was sent back to New York, but no one needed an auxiliary bishop. So the archdiocese had to find him a job. He was put in charge of the annual Peter's Pence Collection for the Holy See. But no one wanted a bishop in charge, so he lost that job. After a long wait he wrote a letter suggesting that it might be scandalous for a bishop to be without work. The answer came back, "Wait." And so he waited. To support himself he finally opened a gasoline station.

Many decades later, Archbishop Francis Spellman was sent to New York. As the story is told, Pope Pius XII asked him to find out what had happened to Bishop Brodrick. No one in the archdiocese had any idea what had happened to the bishop, but they found an old address in a village upstate. Archbishop Spellman drove up to this address. It was a gasoline station. As the story goes, he got out and asked the boy serving gas, "Who owns this gas station?" The boy replied, "Doc Brodrick." The archbishop asked where he lived. The boy indicated a little house nearby. The soon-to-be Cardinal Spellman went over and rang the doorbell, and an older man dressed in overalls came out. "Bishop Brodrick?" The man answered, "Yes." He said, "I'm Archbishop Spellman, and I've come to see if I can do anything for you. The reply was, "Come in. I've been waiting for you for thirty years." Cardinal Spellman made him auxiliary bishop of New York and vicar of religious. I don't know of anyone else who got hurt that badly by the Church. I wonder if someone should look into a possible cause of beatification of Bishop Brodrick and call him patron saint of the patient. Instead of depicting him with a lily or something like that, he could be portrayed holding a gas pump nozzle with that little gadget on the end of it.

How Can the Church of Christ Fail Us?

The question is obvious. How could this happen in a Church founded by Christ? The answer is to be found in the Gospels. What about the apostles? How did they do? Did they fail Jesus Christ when he needed them the most? On the very day when they were made his sacred representatives—the day he told them, "Do this in remembrance of me"—on that day they ran out on him. Every year priests celebrate Holy Thursday as the anniversary of the Catholic priesthood. It is also the anniversary of the day when the first priests failed so terribly. In the early evening they were all made what we have come to call the priests of the New Testament. Later in that evening they ran away. Does that tell you something about the Church? Is it the true Church? Yes. But in this world it is a collection of poor sinners. It will be, as St. Paul says, in eternal life, a Church without spot or wrinkle or any such blemish, but not in this world. "Christ loved the Church and handed himself over for her to sanctify her, cleaning her by the bath of water with the word, that he might present to himself the Church in splendor, without spot or wrinkle or any such thing, that she might be holy and without blemish" (Eph 5:25–27).

The Church is made up of almost a billion people with original sin. That's a whole lot of original sin. And these billion people do extraordinarily good things—and some of them do extraordinarily bad things. If the Catholic Church is the true Church of Christ, you should expect the greatest of saints and the worst of knaves and sinners would be in the same Church. That is what happened in the time of Christ. Some of the fundamentalist churches have the idea that they are going to be the Church of the saints. You have, for example, the Mormons, who call themselves the Church of Jesus Christ of Latter Day Saints.

I was flying out to Salt Lake City, and a man was sitting next to me reading a Mormon book. He was very well dressed, a proper-looking gentleman. He ordered a Scotch on the rocks for lunch, which is a no-no if you're a Mormon. Someone once told me that these people are called "Jack Mormons". It's an interesting phrase. We ought to borrow it, because there are a lot of "Jack Catholics" around. No one lives the Christian life perfectly. This world is filled with absurdities—the world of believers and unbelievers at the same time. In my life I've known dumb Jesuits, confused Dominicans, proud Capuchins, rich Franciscans, and Salesians who can't stand small children. I've known merciless Sisters of Mercy and uncharitable Missionaries of Charity and foolish Daughters of Wisdom. I am, regrettably, a Franciscan of the Renewal who has a long way to go before becoming renewed. Someone asked me one day, "What's so renewed about you?" I had no answer. Go visit Rome. They say it's a city where Communists pray and prelates don't. Everything in this world is a bit messed up, and often it is far better to laugh than to cry. When you have life all figured out, you can be sure that you are overlooking some important pieces of the puzzle. Life is mysterious.

The Church of Latter Day Sinners

I think that the Catholic Church should be called the Church of Latter Day Sinners. That's all we claim to be. There are those churches who feel they are perfect. I feel sorry for them. Jimmy Swaggart had one of those churches going for a while, but he dropped out. Perhaps much for his own spiritual benefit, the bottom fell out. Members of his church all thought they were saints, but it's a good thing that they weren't. Jesus Christ did not come to save the saints. He came to save the sinners. "For I came not to call the righteous, but sinners" (Mt 9:13). Jimmy has announced himself to be a penitent since the time when he ran into disgrace. That was very wise. He should have been doing it all the time. The followers of Jesus Christ are all poor, self-confessed sinners if they are wise. I have been privileged to know a few people who some day may be canonized saints, but they all thought that they were poor sinners.

You must expect that these poor sinners in the Church are going to get hurt and that they are going to hurt each other. To be let down by the Church is not a reason to leave her, anymore than to be let down by your family is a reason to give up family life and move to a desert island. Are there any who have not been hurt by members of their family? In his *City of God*, St. Augustine wisely observed that it breaks the heart of any good person to see that even in one's own home one is not in a safe place and that one may be attacked even there by an enemy posing as a friend or even by an enemy who used to be a loved one.[1] If we all

[1] St. Augustine, *City of God*, book XIX, chap. 5, ed. Vernon Bourke (New York: Doubleday, 1958), 44.

gave up on the human race because we have been hurt, we'd have to move to separate planets.

What to Do

We've all been hurt by people in the Church, even those in authority. When this happens, the first thing to do is to calm down. In fact, that's a good rule when you get hurt by anyone. Take a walk and calm down. The Irish have a saying, "Take counsel with your pillow", which means to sleep on it. Then ask yourself, when you calm down, "Is this really my problem? Did I expect too much from mortal human beings? Am I looking for something in the Church that legitimately I may hope for?" The answer is probably "Yes." It was reasonable, even just. But I cannot absolutely demand kind and faithful treatment, because Jesus Christ himself did not find this in the Church he established. As we have seen, the Church has always been made up of weak individuals. When we are hurt by the Church we recognize that the problem is that "the Church" can be very inconsistent. The people in the Church can be nice one day and bad the next. Even on the same day and in the same parish, there are those who can be terribly charitable and terribly unkind.

Next I ask myself the question, "Am I overly dependent on the Church? Has my reliance on Church people caused me not to rely enough on God and his Son?" You know, many people have very positive experiences in the Church. They work for the Church, and it's been a very positive experience. They went to a Catholic school, and they learned a lot. They were part of a committee or a movement or something in the Church, and it was the most positive thing they ever did in their whole lives. They think that's going to last forever. That's what you call a honeymoon, and it doesn't last. All things pass away. Don't depend on a particular part of the Church. Depend on God.

The Saint Who Wanted Nothing

The life of St. John of the Cross, the Carmelite mystic, is a case in point. This good man was always in trouble. He was a very bright, extremely spiritual and devout man. At the direction of St. Teresa of Avila, he once built a novitiate for the Carmelite friars of her reform. When she went to see it, there were crosses all over the place. She said, "Too many crosses. Take some of them down." She was very direct and much older than St. John of the Cross. Already he had suffered very much for her reform. John of the Cross, when he was in the regular old observance of the Carmelites, was arrested, imprisoned in the monastery, and beaten so severely in the refectory that he carried the scars with him to his grave. He started the new community at the behest of St. Teresa, and after her death his own friars tried to throw him out of the community. St. Teresa could not come to his rescue. Can you imagine?

St. John of the Cross gives this advice to religious: live in the world as if you lived there all by yourself with God. Don't look for anything. Don't get involved in all the comings and goings. Don't have great expectations. Just do what you are supposed to do and say your prayers.[2] That does sound a bit severe, doesn't it? Yet there is more than a grain

---

[2] St. John of the Cross, *Points of Love: The Complete Works of St. John of the Cross*, trans. E. Allison Peers, vol. 3 (Westminster, Md.: Newman Bookshop, 1946), 256.

of truth in it. We always get hurt by the people we love. The people we don't love can't hurt us very much.

St. John of the Cross did not die a bitter man, although his confrères were trying at that point to throw him out of the order on the charge of being stupid—this great Doctor of the Church. I don't know when they ever decided to throw anybody out for being stupid. No one defended John of the Cross. There were all these young friars whom, as novice master, he had trained. He had taught them about the spiritual life, and yet not one of them defended him. I guess you can say that the Church—or the part of the Church that was most important to him—let him down. But he remained calm and at peace. He busied himself in his final assignment by working on his great books and doing pastoral counseling with the lay people, since none of the friars would even listen to him.

The Most Misunderstood Man

And then we come to St. Francis of Assisi. We are all familiar with happy pictures of St. Francis and the friars. To tell the truth, St. Francis lived the last years of his life pretty much in exile. He had few companions, and his order was governed by a man, Elias of Cortona, who was really his worst enemy. Elias did not even die a Franciscan.

St. Francis suffered because very few people really shared his vision. Some of his followers, not able to live up to his incredible example, slipped into silly rationalizations. Others slid the other way into fanaticism. Some chose this and others chose that as the part of his message they would emphasize. In the end almost all deserted him, and yet they all cried at his funeral. Stuck between indulgence and arrogance, sentimentality and fanaticism, they never really understood this holy man, who saw himself as very simple. In the end he got hurt by those who in fact loved him but did not understand him. We learn from both St. John of the Cross and St. Francis not to depend too much on any particular part of the Church but to put our trust in God.

If you get hurt by the Church, sit down and ask yourself, "Did I forget that the Church was made up of human beings with original sin? Did I forget that she is a great dragnet cast into the sea? Did I forget that at any given time in the Church you can find some of the best and some of the worst people?" Begin to look at the Church differently. St. Francis, speaking about the possibility of being persecuted by the clergy, wrote:

> God inspired me, too, and still inspires me with such great faith in priests who live according to the laws of the holy Church of Rome, because of their dignity, that if they persecuted me, I should still be ready to turn to them for aid. And if I were as wise as Solomon and met the poorest priests of the world, I would still refuse to preach against their will in the parishes in which they live. I am determined to reverence, love and honour priests and all others as my superiors. I refuse to consider their sins, because I can see the Son of God in them and they are better than I. I do this because in this world I cannot see the most high Son of God with my own eyes, except for his most holy Body and Blood which they receive and they alone administer to others.[3]

When to Move

Sometimes people come to me and say, "I can't stand my parish. The sermons are not really authentic teaching of the

---

[3] *The Testament of St. Francis: Omnibus of Sources*, ed. Marion Habig (Chicago: Franciscan Herald Press, 1988), 67.

Catholic faith." Sadly, this can happen in these times. It has happened before in Church history. When you consider that only one of the thirty bishops in England remained loyal to the Church at the time of Henry VIII, it's quite possible that you could go to a Catholic Church and hear what is not authentic Catholic teaching. And people ask me, "What do I do?" If you have a car, drive. If you don't have one, either get one or a bicycle, or a horse, or hitch a ride with a friend. Move, or buy bus tokens. Go someplace else. This is a world of transportation. If you are in a parish where you are uncomfortable because you think the people in charge are not enthusiastically loyal to the teaching of the Catholic Church presently interpreted by the Bishop of Rome, move. People always ask me, "What should I do?" Travel.

Make Your Voice Heard

If things aren't that bad, but are disquieting, make an intelligent noise. Unfortunately, most of the time the noises that people make are not very intelligent. I learned this because sometimes I have to follow up on complaints, and at least half the complaints are just off the deep end. They're silly or trivial or crazy. At times good complaints are submitted, but the one complaining arrives with an axe. You're trying to do the best you can to keep the local Church going, trying to represent the Mystical Body of Christ in the messy world we live in, and someone is all upset because a priest wears blue vestments in Advent or something like that. Many devout but troubled Catholics don't know how to make the distinction between someone being heretical and someone being naughty.

The Time I Broke the Rules

At times people get too upset about small things. If you're a
priest, sooner or later you're going to have to break a rule
for the good of souls. The breaking of a rule is by no means
always a sin. In fact, it may be a sin not to break the rule.
The rules of the Church, even the canons, often admit of
excusing causes. I'll give you an example of my breaking a
fairly serious rule. At the same time, I even committed a
legal misdemeanor. I was to celebrate Mass for the fiftieth
wedding anniversary of a very devout, lovely Puerto Rican
couple. They had children, grandchildren, and great-
grandchildren, all baptized and confirmed—a marvelous
family. I showed up the day before the big celebration and
asked, "Is tomorrow actually the anniversary?" Dead silence.
There were about twelve relatives in the room. I said,
"Well, what was the exact date? Do you remember the day
you got married, so I can mention it in my sermon tomorrow?" Finally, one of the daughters spoke up and said,
"Padre, they was married by God." Well, who am I that I
should improve on what God has done? They were poor
people, and they never went through a ceremony, so instead of this being simply an anniversary, I was to do a wedding. A rule both of the Church and state is that a
clergyman cannot perform a wedding without a civil marriage license. To do so is a misdemeanor. So, fifty years late,
I called up the chancery office and said, "Listen, it's three
o'clock in the afternoon, and there're going to be about a
hundred people here tomorrow; if you think I'm going to
drive this old couple down to city hall and get them a Was-
sermann Test, you have another thought coming." This
chancery official, now a bishop, simply said, "Be sure to get

delegation from the pastor to make it a valid Church wedding." I performed the wedding without the civil license. They can come and take me away. If this is discovered, I'll never be an attorney general. I've publicly confessed the only misdemeanor I know I've committed.

Christians May Not Be Pharisees

We must not be Pharisees. The Pharisees did not do well. They spent plenty of time and energy observing the law, but they missed the Son of God. They were there on Calvary, but they were on the wrong side.

On the other hand, we must be honest and people of integrity. It is necessary to know the difference between a dogma and a tradition. If you're going to object to something that's out of order, you need to know how important it really is. I was castigated as a young priest in the sixties when, with the written permission of the archbishop, I preached in synagogues and Protestant churches. People made fun of me, criticized me, wrote to the chancery office against me, and all the time I had the permission of Cardinal Spellman. I lived to see Pope John Paul II preach in the synagogue of Rome. I was severely criticized for doing something that within twenty years the Pope himself would do.

These are difficult times, times of change. We need to keep our priorities in right order. If you dissent or complain, do so wisely, charitably, and well. It is wise and charitable to make a distinction between an abuse, an exception, and a personal peeve. Some devout people need to remember that Christ does not exist for the Church; the Church exists for and with Christ. He is the Supreme Shepherd of the Church. The Holy Father is not the Supreme Shepherd of the Church, but rather the Vicar of Christ. He stands in his place in this world. Christ is the Supreme Shepherd—not only in the days when he walked this earth, but by divine providence and the inspiration of the Holy Spirit he is the Shepherd of the Church today. He guides his Church. It is people in the Church who mess things up. The apostles did not do well even when Christ was alive. They fumbled and made mistakes even though he was there. This fumbling will continue to the end of the world. I suggest that you be patient with the leaders of the Church, because we are in extremely difficult, confusing, and pagan times. It is important not to disturb the peace of the Church unnecessarily.

I've given retreats to a couple of hundred bishops. They have a very difficult role. Just like you and me, they were, for the most part, not prepared for the times we live in. Most of them grew up in times when religion was a very positive and accepted part of American life. Religion was popular and had great influence on the culture.

We have all come to live in totally unexpected times and to see things that we never even imagined. I have seen elderly religious sisters, in their seventies and eighties, arrested because they were protesting in front of places where children were killed. And I said to myself, "Is this the United States?" I have visited priests and bishops in prison. My friends Bishop Austin Vaughn and Bishop George Lynch both went to jail for several days. In Bishop Lynch's case, it was for several weeks. Again I ask the question, "Is this happening in the United States?" They and other clergy and religious were in prison for protesting something that was a serious crime in the United States only a few decades ago. People who performed abortions twenty-five years ago were felons. The American Medical Association excoriated them as low-life for taking the lives of unborn children—and suddenly this is not only accepted but paid for by the taxpayer.

Being Loyal Even When You Are Hurt

There are huge dangers looming over the Church now. What loyal Christians need is a perspective. Those who complain about the music while the Church is facing the hurricane that is breaking over us remind me of passengers playing shuffleboard on the deck of the *Titanic*. It is a time to be faithful to the Church. I worked for Terence Cardinal Cooke, a man who loved the Catholic Church. Like his predecessor, Cardinal Spellman, and his successor, Cardinal O'Connor, he labored for it endlessly, "in journeying often and in many sleepless nights" (2 Cor 11:26–27). He pushed himself beyond every level of human expectation, even when he was dying. He loved all of God's people, not only Catholics. He loved Orthodox Christians, Protestants, Jews, Muslims. When he became archbishop he said, "I recognize my responsibility as bishop of all the people in this city, even those who do not believe at all in God. I will serve as best I can if they will let me serve them." Yet I heard him preach these words in St. Patrick's Cathedral: "Let us love our Church. Let us work for the Church. Let us suffer for the Church and defend the Church."

Perhaps the Church has hurt you. The Church has hurt me. It has hurt most people near it for any length of time—not the whole Church, but part of it. I assure you that you and I will know, at the end of our days, that great Church which is the Mystical Body of Christ when it comes to its full reality. That is what eternal life is—when all who are saved from every nation and race and people will be gathered into the Mystical Body of Christ. We are preparing now for the heavenly Church, but our own spiritual life will be very weak and very narrow indeed if we do not loyally struggle for the Church in this world and try to be faithful to her even when others are not faithful. On Judgment Day no one is going to ask you about what anybody else did for the Church, only about what you and I did as individuals, as members of the Church of Christ in this wounded world. St. Paul, who loved the Church and suffered for her, writes to us,

> I rejoice in my suffering for your sake, and in my flesh I complete what is lacking in Christ's afflictions for the sake of his body, that is, the church, of which I became a minister according to the divine office which was given to me for you, to make the word of God fully known, the mystery hidden for ages and generations but now made manifest to his saints (Col 1:24–28).

Let us be faithful to that Church which our Lord Jesus Christ sent down through the ages, and let us find our spiritual fulfillment in being what St. Francis, St. Catherine, St. Teresa, St. John of the Cross, St. Pius X, Padre Pio, Father Solanus, Cardinal Cooke, Pope John Paul II, and Mother Teresa all were or are in their lives—faithful, humble, generous, self-effacing members of the Church of Christ.

— *Prayer* —

O LORD JESUS CHRIST, when you walked this earth you experienced much rejection . . . the rejection of your family in Nazareth and of the people you met in Israel, and also the betrayal of your own apostles. This did not deter you, even though you wept over Jerusalem and deeply regretted the failure of your friends. You loved them even unto the end. You also gave us the Church and called it your Church. You suffered and died for the mystical reality we call your body, the union of all those who in eternal life will be saved and united with you. Help us, O Lord, when the Church on earth fails us. Help us not to be bitter, not to be rebellious, not to expect much, but, following your own example and the example of your saints, let us love and not rebel. Help us to accept and correct without bitterness. Help us to serve and not to expect a reward. In this difficult time, shed your grace upon the children of your Church so that we may withstand the attacks and scandals of our time. By your grace call those who are the enemies of your Church to be her friends and members, as you once called Paul to be the servant of the Church. And help us, O Lord, in the midst of all this confusion, to believe in your own words spoken through the apostles to the whole Church, "And behold I am with you until the end of the world." Amen.

5

When We Are
Our Own Worst Enemies

We have considered the problems that we may have with others and our difficulties with the Church. Now we must look at the problems we have with ourselves. You may find that if you look into your own life (especially as you get older) one of the most important realizations in the process of maturation is that we bring many, if not most, of our problems on ourselves. When things don't make sense, it's often because we didn't make sense out of things. There may be some consolation in knowing that this is a general human experience. One finds the tendency to make troubles for oneself even in the lives of saints. Like the rest of us, even these special people brought on many of their own troubles. Few are exempt from being their own enemies at least some of the time. Saints, sinners, biblical personages, and even modern celebrities all gather together under the great banner that says: "Let's sink our own boat." It's one of the more obvious and universal signs of original sin that with a series of well thought out moves, carefully considered, prudently studied, and done with great expeditiousness and even prayer, we sink our boats, saints and sinners alike.

In many cases, one has to be a bit of a sinner to be one's own worst enemy. However, it is not by any means necessary. You can do this just as effectively even if you're devout—you will just do it a bit more piously. We can all say with a certain amount of conviction that "we've met the enemy and it's us".

Stepping Out in Faith

Just think of some of the ways a person can mess up things for himself. The most obvious is precipitous behavior—going ahead and doing something and not considering the implications, all of the things that are going to be consequential from it. Many devout people say, "I can't figure it out, so I'm going to take the great leap of faith and jump . . . into an empty swimming pool." I hear people saying, "I'm going to step out in faith!" Why don't they step out in common sense at the same time? Don't blame God if you walk off the end of the dock.

The opposite mistake is thinking things out so carefully and being so cautious that we don't do what we're supposed to do. As Christians we are supposed to step out in faith, but we often sit down in confusion. Many, not knowing what to do, simply don't do anything. I call this dangerous trait the *Titanic* phenomenon. On the *Titanic* that mild winter's night when the sea was very calm and the great ship had struck an iceberg, many prudent people didn't get into the lifeboats. They said to themselves, "This is a great ship; it can't possibly sink." Although there were not enough lifeboats for all, there were nonetheless two hundred empty seats in the lifeboats when the *Titanic* went down. I suppose some who got into the lifeboats must have said to themselves, "I'm going to look terribly stupid when they pull this lifeboat back up onto the ship in about six hours, and I've been out here in the sea." But these people watched as the great ship went down. It's hard to know what to do. You can pray very fervently and still make big mistakes. What is more mysterious is that when we make big mistakes good things happen anyway. It's not easy to be a responsible human being. The forgotten reason for all this is original sin.

Denial of Reality

Another effective way to sink one's boat is to deny obvious dangers and walk into them. In psychology we speak about defense mechanisms, unconscious ways of distorting realities we think we can't cope with. Consider the successful professional who is smoking two packs a day. He has been told a thousand times, "That's very dangerous for your health." He may reply, "You know, Golda Meir used to smoke two packs a day, and she lived into her seventies." This chain smoker ignores the army of other people who smoked two packs a day and who didn't make it to fifty. We all deny obvious dangers. At this time there are appalling cracks and rifts in the Church, many signs of disunity. Yet, responsible people often deny these dangers. They pretend they're not there. The same could be said for the Western-style democracies and their ignoring of the demands and plights of the Third World.

Some years ago, a study was done of vocational recruitment policies of religious communities in the United States. I wrote to the well-known religious agency that sponsored this study. The priest who conducted the study was quite objective and consequently very critical of the vocational program. The person at the office who answered my phone call maintained that the study had never been done. However, I had read about it in several newspapers at the time. The author had opened his report by saying there was only one word to describe present vocational recruitment, "catas-trophic". All the orders he studied told him that they had the best vocational recruitment program. But there was no one in these programs! This is called denial. The defense mechanism of denial is one of the more dangerous forms of human behavior. It was Neville Chamberlain, the Prime Minister of England, who came home from his meeting with Hitler and said, "There will be peace in our time." He denied the obvious evidence of his senses.

There are people around who say that the Church is doing wonderfully. They're all filled with happiness. Look out the porthole. The blue stuff you see is not sky. It's water. The decks are awash. We've lost about 50 percent of the practicing Catholics in thirty years. Whatever else is going on, this trend is not good. The great religious orders that trained many of us are on the verge of extinction. But they think that they're doing wonderfully.

How to Avoid Being Our Own Worst Enemies

Failure to organize our behavior around our everlasting goal and our God-appointed purpose in life makes us the fools that Christ speaks about in the parables. We should organize our lives around eternity to avoid self-destruction. I'm not saying that everybody should enter the cloister. That's a rare vocation. But I am saying that whatever we do, no matter what evaluation other people may make, we should con-sciously and purposely live every day so that it contributes to our salvation. An example may help. I have written the letters of dispensation for more than a hundred eighty priests. I may hold the world record—it's part of my job. Sometimes these men had to leave. It was the only course of action open to them that was honest and moral. But I always say to a priest as we finish up our interviews, "Whatever you do, do this for your salvation. No one else may understand it, but leave for your salvation. Fit it into your spiritual life." Many look at me very puzzled when I say this because, in our society, about the ninety-ninth thing in the order of importance is salvation. The vast majority of things that go on in the world about us have nothing to do with salvation. Yet salvation is the only task that we have set before us that will last forever. Our Lord says this very clearly, "What does it profit a man, to gain the whole world and to forfeit his life?" (Mk 8:36). Clearly, one of the highways to self-destructiveness is to fail to organize your behavior around your eternal salvation.

Another Road Down: Going against God

Another popular road to self-destruction is indulgence in things that are forbidden. I know many who say they would like to do God's will and really consider themselves Christian, but . . . then comes the fine print. Of course we all sin, and sin often, out of weakness, concupiscence, feebleness, and confusion. We may even, in a stupid moment, sin with deliberate will. But knowingly and deliberately to stay on a course of action that one knows is contrary to the law of God is to open oneself for disaster. This is a commitment to sin. Many writers—from St. Paul to Shakespeare to the novelist Flannery O'Connor—have said the same thing: "How blest are they that walk according to the law of the Lord and how unblest are they who do not."

Even some believers in our time don't want to hear this truth. I know a priest who was called down to headquarters for telling people certain things were sins, acts that the Church teaches are sinful. He was told by authorities that he was being negative in his sermons. Let's stop the nonsense! It's extremely self-destructive for Christians to gainsay, go ahead of, change, or alter the law of God, either directly, by saying "God doesn't really mean that", or indirectly, by interpreting the law of God in such a way as to make it meaningless.

The Catholic Church has become a counter-culture religion in the United States. One of the newspapers generally guilty of Catholic-bashing ran an editorial recently against Catholic-bashing. The editor called Catholic-bashers scoundrels. Let me tell you, he ought to look in a mirror. He announced that the only group in the United States that anyone could be respectfully prejudiced against was Catholics. I would have extended that to evangelical Protestants and Orthodox Jews. We're all in the same boat. And we could all easily get the pressure off us if we just shut up about abortion and the social acceptance of homosexual behavior as the equivalent of marriage and if we kept quiet about euthanasia. We don't have to agree with the secularists. We just have to keep quiet, roll over, and play dead. Yet in the long run, such behavior would be extraordinarily destructive to the Church.

I was amused recently at the annual controversy over the St. Patrick's Day parade in New York City and whether the gay demonstrators could walk—not that they give a hoot for St. Patrick. In response to this nonsense, a group of Orthodox Jews announced that if the militant gays were allowed to walk in the St. Patrick's Day parade, the Orthodox Jews would walk in the gay liberation parade carrying big signs that read "SODOMY IS A SIN". That's an example of being affirmative rather than self-destructive.

Many of the movers and shakers in the Church are counseling a prudent acceptance of the wrong direction that the
United States has taken in recent decades. I am reminded of
the old saying of the pagan philosophers: "The mills of the
gods grind slowly, but they grind exceedingly fine." There
is also a statement in Scripture, "How blest are they whose
way is blameless, who walk in the law of the Lord" (Ps
119:1). And in the New Testament, there are the words of
our Savior, "Everyone who acknowledges me before men, I
also will acknowledge before my Father who is in heaven"
(Mt 10:32).

There are many other admonitions in the New Testament, especially those of our Lord and St. Paul, counseling
us not to conform ourselves to the spirit of the world. Con-
formity to this disintegrating world is the core message contained in much of the media hype that pours out of the
secular sector and even out of the religious establishment.
"Do not be conformed", St. Paul says, "to this world"
(Rom 12:2), because "he who sows to his own flesh will
reap corruption" (Gal 6:8). If there is anything obvious in
the New Testament, it is that to compromise with the values of the world is not only to betray God, but to defeat
your own cause, to bring down upon yourself all kinds of
disasters, not from God but from self.

Christians ought to read the history of what the churches
did in Germany at the time of the rise of Hitler. Many of
them kept quiet, assuming that a madman could never stay
in power. Even Pope Pius XI, assuming that Hitler was
going to go under soon, signed a concordat with Germany,
but later he admitted that he was wrong. Don't ever say that
popes can't be wrong about such things. In 1937, Pope Pius
XI wrote an encyclical against Hitler, the first words of
which indicated that he had misjudged the situation. He

began with the words, "It is with deep anxiety and growing surprise that We have long been following the painful trials of the Church and the increasing vexations which afflict those who have remained loyal in heart and action. . . ." [1] Pope Pius regretted what he had done at first, but he did not keep quiet after that. He condemned the Nazis and their anti-Semitism in the clearest terms.

Pity Parties and Resentment Reunions

Another very effective way to defeat yourself is to keep alive all kinds of hurt feelings. The Pharaohs of Egypt used to collect their tears in vials and keep them in sacred places. They were buried in the pyramids with their tears. The Pharaohs aren't the only ones. If you want to live on resentment and hurt feelings, you'll have an unhealthy diet for the rest of your life, pure psychological cholesterol. How many people spend much of their energy lamenting, crying, being unhappy or sad or driving themselves literally crazy by living on resentments toward those who failed them? Yes, people do fail us. Some don't even know they're failing us; some don't mean to fail us. Some are so preoccupied with their own problems, they don't even know what they're doing. And some just don't care. The motto of the follower of Christ must be, "Keep going ahead. Don't look back." If our Lord Jesus Christ had been someone preoccupied with his own hurt feelings, none of us would have been saved. Mercifully, God does not nurse hurt feelings. For our own spiritual, as well as psychological, good, we must forgive those who trespass against us.

[1] Pope Pius XI, *Mit brennender Sorge* (On the Present Position of the Catholic Church in the German Empire), March 1937.

Waging War against Oneself

We all get involved in something that has a peculiar psychological name, "passive aggression". It's very insidious. We don't know we're doing ourselves in, but we set ourselves up for disaster unconsciously. We get involved in something good or bad that's going nowhere. There are people who make a career out of being passive-aggressive. As you lend them your car, you know that they're going to wreck it, and they do. You need someone to go get more ice cream for the party, and one of these people is the nearest person. You hand him the money, saying, "Go, get a few gallons of inexpensive ice cream." He returns with pickles because they were on sale. Whose mistake was it in the first place? Yours!

We can all be self-destructive for the most efficient reasons. Here's an example. Because of my heart condition I take an anticoagulant. If I get a bruise, it quickly becomes a hematoma. These are most unpleasant. They swell up and last for weeks. I was told to put heat on one that I had not too long ago. Since I like to do things efficiently and quickly, I went to the drugstore and discovered the new microwave heat packs. These packs have all kinds of warnings on them. "Be careful, watch out. Make sure there are other people around. Don't use this too long." When I took the pack from the microwave, it didn't feel very hot. I put it on, and I got four second-degree burns. They say the best thing to do with a burn is leave it exposed to the air. So then the burns got infected. I went six times to doctors and needed antibiotics. Why did I do this to myself? To save time. I intensely dislike taking medication or going to drugstores. I don't even mind the thought of dying, but I just don't want it to take too long (just long enough to do my video series on getting ready for death). Because I was saving time, I ended up visiting all these nice doctors in several different cities. The thing that finally helped me the most was an old faithful, hydrogen peroxide. It's cheaper than bottled water. Hidden behind this stupid experience was a bit of self-destructiveness, I have no doubt. It was all too well thought out to be an accident. I say to myself, "I was an infirmarian for years. I know how to do bandages. I know all about infections. I know about microbes. How did I do this?" I did it to myself because I am regularly unconcerned about my health.

Misery, masochism—don't kid yourself. When you find yourself clearly behind the eight ball, sit down and examine the unconscious planning you did to accomplish your predicament so effectively. This kind of self-destruction is often seen in the Bible. Moses, that great holy man, ends up making his brother Aaron the high priest. Aaron must have been an idiot. Moses goes up on Mt. Sinai to meet God. The place is blowing up—thunder, lightning, earthquakes—and what is brother Aaron doing? He's building a golden calf out of earrings. He must have really been stupid. And Moses, of course, was not passive-aggressive himself, so when he came down the mountain, he broke the calf up, burned it, and made Aaron and his boys drink the ashes in bitter water. This was not passive-aggressive; it was active-aggressive. How did he ever get involved with this idiot?

Another Old Testament saint was always setting himself up for disaster—Jonah, the prophet. God finally tells him to stop belly-aching. "For heaven's sake, Jonah, you didn't even plant that vine that died. You're feeling sorry for yourself" (Jon 4:10 freely translated).

I occasionally give retreats to bishops. I used to give more, but in my old age I'm getting a little too honest, so I don't get as many invitations now. Bishops, as you may not know, are a very battered and beat-up group. When I give a retreat to the bishops, I have to be quite gentle because they know better than anybody else how miserable things really are. Years ago, bishops never heard the truth. Now they never hear anything good or even nice. Whenever I give a retreat to bishops, I try to remind them that they are the successors of the apostles. But remember what happened to the apostles. The twelve apostles were there for the great Passover of the New Testament, and they ran away. They ran away! Doesn't that tell you something? St. Augustine always reminded his fellow bishops that one does not necessarily become impeccable upon becoming a bishop. Bishops have to watch out more than anyone else because from those to whom much is given, much is expected.

In the New Testament, we find many examples of people who sank their own boats—St. Peter, Judas, the high priests. The high priests missed the Messiah because they were being expedient. Aren't we humans peculiar creatures? I suspect that both Peter and Judas, on the one hand, and the high priests, on the other, were operating on resentment. Peter and Judas resented our Lord's not setting himself up as a secular messiah. Jesus didn't come to Jerusalem and turn the gates of the temple to gold and the spears of the Roman soldiers to butter. He stayed up in Galilee, healing all of those lepers and Cyro-Phoenicians and preaching in places like Naim, which to this day doesn't have a main street. Peter and Judas said, "Why don't you go down to Jerusalem? What are you doing up here?" And then when he finally decided to go to Jerusalem it was the wrong time as far as they were concerned. They resented Jesus because he went down even though he knew he was going to be killed.

The unbeliever may ask an interesting question. Was Jesus self-destructive? There are forms of piety and devotion that seem to suggest that he was. I think some people project their own powerful self-destructiveness on our Lord. They make him sound self-destructive, but this is biblically and theologically absurd. Our Lord pleaded with the people to accept him, didn't he? He tried to convert them, and if he had succeeded in converting the world, we would have been saved by his life and not by his death. But when he realized in his human life (he mysteriously always knew it in his divine intelligence) that they were not going to accept him, then he boldly faced the inevitable, which the apostles could not face. "Behold, we are going up to Jerusalem, and the Son of man will be delivered to the chief priests and scribes, and they will condemn him to death, and deliver him to the Gentiles to be mocked and scourged and crucified, and he will be raised on the third day" (Mt 20:18–19). Don't ever forget those last phrases, because by the most terrible tortures and dying he accomplished all things.

There are authors around who try to interpret Jesus as merely a human being, forgetting his divinity, and then he sounds self-destructive. Our Lord did not suffer from the pathologies that fallen human beings experience. He wanted to be accepted in order to convert the world. Since that was not possible, he accepted the lot of all good human beings who fail. He did not seek to free himself from the inevitability that he would be tortured and killed. The human race, in its fallen state, always hates and kills two kinds of people, the very bad and the very good. They are the most vulnerable.

The Most Tragic Figure of All

Perhaps the saddest figure of all is Judas. We forget that Judas was one of the apostles. With sincerity and enthusiasm, he once chose to follow the Messiah. We may speculate that he misunderstood Christ, but so did the rest of them. Judas had the marvelous opportunity, right on the threshold of disaster, to turn back. When Christ said to him, "Do you betray the Son of man with a kiss?", he could have said, "No!" He could have turned and said to the soldiers, "Go home; you're all fools." Then, instead of throwing the money into the temple, he would have thrown it at the priests. He could have gone with Jesus up to the Sanhedrin and to Pontius Pilate and said, "I surrendered an innocent man. He did not do the things that he is accused of." Our Lord might have been set free by Pilate. His enemies would have had to catch him another time. We would have several more parables, a few more miracles, a few more precious pages in the Gospels. But Judas remained his own worst enemy even to the end, walking past the place of the crucifixion to hang himself. He had to walk near Calvary, since the whole area is not very large. Having destroyed his reputation, the whole engagement of his life, he could have turned around and gone to Calvary and knelt at the foot of the Cross and asked for forgiveness. Every artist in the world would have painted the scene. There would be a picture of the scene in almost every church, St. Judas Iscariot kneeling next to John at the foot of the Cross. In every large city there would be a large church named St. Judas the Penitent. His reputation would be the theme of much literature. His conversion is the page that is not written, because Judas destroyed himself—out of self-hatred, out of resentment, out of hopelessness.

Down through the history of the Church you find many well-intentioned people who, often out of the best of motives, hurt the cause to which they have assigned their best energies. Often they are very well intentioned and actually close to God, but saints can make big mistakes, too. For example, St. Francis made a terrible mistake in his life. He did it out of good will and naïveté. He let in every Tom, Dick, and Harry who came along and wanted to join his order. At the end of his life there were five thousand men in the order, and perhaps half of them should have gone home. They betrayed St. Francis. They elected his worst enemy, Elias, general in his place. He let in too many men too easily. Don't think that only sinners make mistakes.

The saintly Pope Pius V excommunicated Queen Elizabeth I of England. She had never been raised a Catholic, but she had been baptized a Catholic. By excommunicating her, Pius absolved the English Catholics of their responsibility of allegiance to the Queen, putting them into the position of possibly being traitors. Initially Elizabeth herself did not have strong anti-Catholic feelings. But she was put in a political situation by a pope who was very saintly but who many think did the wrong thing. English Catholics are likely to tell you he made a lot of martyrs unnecessarily.

The history of the Catholic Church in the United States is filled with dumb moves. A century ago, thousands of immigrants from Ukraine and Carpathia came to the United States. They belonged to the Ukrainian and Ruthenian Rite of the Catholic Church. By ancient custom, their diocesan priests were allowed to marry and raise families. At that time there were no Eastern Rite dioceses, so these devout immigrants were cared for by Latin Rite bishops. Some of the more conservative bishops, mostly Irish and German immigrants themselves, went along and accepted the tradition of married priests even though they found it foreign to their experience. However, the leader of the Americanizing movement in the Church, Archbishop John Ireland of St. Paul (then considered a great progressive), so badly treated the Eastern Rite Catholics that hundreds of thousands of them left the Church and became Orthodox. I have often heard Archbishop Ireland called the founder of the Orthodox Church in America, because he lacked a broad vision of the Church.

I once knew a great cardinal very well who would be the first in the world to admit that he made mistakes. His two favorite phrases were "Thank you" and "I'm sorry." Cardinal Cooke had no problem with admitting mistakes. He would laugh at himself. Almost his last words to me in this world were, "It was my fault; I didn't make my position clear." To recognize that one may make mistakes, even to accept that these could have been avoided, is ultimately to recognize that one is human. That is the beginning of a way out of self-defeat.

Coping with Self-Defeating Habits

What do we do with our own self-destructive tendencies? The first and obvious thing is to admit that we may indeed be self-destructive. If you think you can't be your own worst enemy, you are easily deceived. To think that you cannot be deceived is to be already deceived, wisely observed St. John of the Cross.

The first thing to do is to try to recognize those tendencies in yourself and cope with them. Trying to get rid of all self-defeating ways is probably a waste of time. But trying to curb and control these tendencies is an effective way to deal with them. Unfortunately, when we try to curb self-defeating tendencies, we inevitably run into the well-meant opposition of our friends. I'm an old-fashioned, card-carrying workaholic. I do certain things to moderate this vice. I take an hour or two off to do something interesting or educational. I may go away and give a retreat so I can get a little peace and normal sleep. Inevitably someone comes along and says, "Oh, you shouldn't do that", or else suggests or demands activity that will be burdensome. Oftentimes I observe this attitude with parents and children. Parents trying to do their best usually have a few self-defeating tendencies, and the children accidentally reinforce these. Mother is worn-out, and she needs a few minutes off. Sure enough one of the kids will say, "Humph, you weren't there when I needed you." I chose the role of mother to illustrate this point because it is really the most demanding role of all. But we can choose any other—father, doctor, teacher, pastor. Someone always has to be available in certain situations, but it does not always have to be the same person. Even mothers desire and need some time off. Once, in a psychology class, we were told that mothers should always be there for the children. I thought to myself, "If mother is always available, she'll soon fall apart."

God Works with Us

God is infinitely good, and he works with our self-destructiveness. He doesn't encourage it in any way, although his representatives may accidentally do so. Christ says, "Love your neighbor as yourself", which makes the assumption that you are not to hate yourself and should not be destroying yourself. However, on the other hand, if after a series of well-placed moves you find yourself going down the chute, God will be there for you. He never, ever gives up on those who let him help them. He remains there to help us even if we (wrongly) blame the problems that we have caused on him. Often we do our own will and convince ourselves that it was God's will. It was not God's will. We were like the safecracker who heard the police outside and knelt down to pray that he wouldn't get caught. We can't expect God to bail us out when we do stupid things, but we can look for him to be there when we acknowledge what we have done. He will be there. Our heavenly Father knows far better than we do that we all have neurotic and self-destructive impulses. He will be sorry for our childishness. He will remain by us. Don't ever expect to do anything perfectly, except to be perfectly stupid, but do expect that whoever calls on the name of the Lord will find him. The Lord said to Moses when he led the Israelites out of Egypt, "Be not frightened, neither be dismayed; for the Lord your God is with you. . . . Behold I send an angel before you to guard you on the way. . . . If you hearken attentively to his voice and do all that I say, then I will be an enemy to your enemies and an adversary to your adversaries" (Jos 1:9, Ex 23:20, 22). But Moses made his mistakes. Did God abandon him? No. St. Peter made his mistakes. Did God abandon him? No. No matter what we do, God will be there. He is immensely merciful and kind.

Our Father Will Be Sorry for Our Childishness

We call God our Father because he has revealed this title. Our Lord uses this title often—although it is certainly true that the heavenly Father is not a male human being, and it is equally true that he embodies the qualities of both mother and father to us all. We call him Father, but we are afraid to let him be a Father. We can't quite understand that like any true father, he will deal with our childishness, our mistakes, even our foolishness with mercy. There is a poem that brings out the loving kindness of God the Father very beautifully. It was written in the latter part of the nineteenth century by a devout Catholic poet, Coventry Patmore, whose wife had recently died, leaving him to raise his family, including his young son, the subject of this poem. I think you will learn much from it about God.

THE TOYS

My little Son, who look'd from thoughtful eyes
And moved and spoke in quiet grown-up wise,
Having my law the seventh time disobey'd,
I struck him, and dismiss'd
With hard words and unkiss'd,
His Mother, who was patient, being dead.
Then, fearing lest his grief should hinder sleep,
I visited his bed,
But found him slumbering deep,
With darken'd eyelids, and their lashes yet
From his late sobbing wet.
And I, with moan,
Kissing away his tears, left others of my own;
For, on a table drawn beside his head,
He had put, within his reach,
A box of counters and a red-vein'd stone,
A piece of glass abraded by the beach,
And six or seven shells,
A bottle with bluebells,

And two French copper coins, ranged there
    with careful art,
To comfort his sad heart.
So when that night I pray'd
To God, I wept, and said:
Ah, when at last we lie with trancèd breath,
Not vexing Thee in death,
And Thou rememberest of what toys
We made our joys,
How weakly understood
Thy great commanded good,
Then fatherly not less
Than I whom Thou has molded from the clay,
Thou'lt leave Thy wrath, and say,
"I will be sorry for their childishness." [2]

If we seek him sincerely and desire to please him above all things, God will accept and work with the mistakes that each one of us makes, saint or sinner. Often these require forgiveness; and his merciful embrace is always there for us even in the worst of times. I know people who have ruined their whole lives but then found God in prison. God was there for them. And so this strange topic of self-defeat, so often experienced, so seldom discussed, ends on this note, "Do not be afraid . . . for the Lord your God is with you" (Jos 1:9). If this is not clear enough, Jesus said to his confused and self-destructive apostles, "Let not your hearts be troubled nor be afraid" (Jn 14:27). "Behold I am with you till the end of the world" (Mt 28:20). No matter what happens, believe that this is true.

---

[2] Coventry Patmore, "The Toys", *Anthology of Catholic Poets*, ed. Joyce Kilmer (Garden City, N.Y.: Doubleday, Image Books, 1955), 195.

— *Prayer* —

HEAVENLY FATHER, I do not pray to you very often in my own words, but use instead the prayer given to us by your own Son. Now, aware of my own self-destructiveness, my own tendency to make the very mistakes I intend to avoid, I turn to you for help. Your wisdom knows, beyond what we can think, that we are the children of a fallen race, that we carry mysterious burdens that cause us to harm or even destroy the very things that would bring us joy and peace. You have sent your only Son to rescue us all, even those who conspired to destroy him. Although I love and trust him, I wonder what I would have done if I would have been among those he challenged and called beyond their narrow, selfish concerns. Nothing in my life convinces me that I would have been among the few who stood by him. And so, I admit, I often fail him even now and leave unused and discarded the chances he gives me better to serve him and those in need, who represent him so well. Father, be with me when I fail you and fail those you have given to me to serve. Right my wrongs. Enlighten my darkness. Straighten out my ways. And be patient with my foolishness. I don't ask you to prevent my mistakes but to help me be patient with others, as you are patient with me. Amen.

6

When Death Robs Us

We come inevitably to the most painful topic in this book, the one that causes believers to waver a bit in their firmness of faith and makes many of the weak stumble. The death of those who are dear to us, of those on whom we have relied, is life's worst pain. We must consider, at the same time, the inevitability of death—the death of those we love and our own deaths. The first thing that must be said is that it is absolutely fruitless to run away from death. There is no place to run. Every one of us, from the youngest to the eldest, is dying at exactly the same speed: twenty-four hours a day, seven days a week. We are all moving through life accompanied by the ticking of the clock. To run from death, to pretend for a time that it doesn't exist, is an utterly useless deception. Death needs to be faced and faced very squarely wherever and whoever you are.

This is not an easy thing to do, for almost everything in our culture pretends that things have to work out well and that there are no mysteries or unsolvable problems. Everything in our culture tells us to pretend that death will not come to us—although, paradoxically, the media are preoccupied by accounts of murder, war, and violent death. Ernest Becker, in his book *The Denial of Death*,[1] analyzed modern American attitudes toward death and concluded that much of our culture is simply a pretense that everyone

[1] Ernest Becker, *The Denial of Death* (New York: Free Press, 1973).

except ourselves is going to die. Somehow or other, you and I are not included—so the illusion goes.

A friend of mine who is a funeral director told me that the "in" people—the well-off and the sophisticated—request that the dead be wrapped up in the bed-clothes in which they died and taken immediately to the crematorium, and the ashes disposed of without any funeral service. They simply disappear. It's as if they never were. This is the "très posh" funeral. Isn't it awful?

But what is almost as bad is to go to a religious funeral that's more like a wedding. Everybody is so happy, Alleluias all over the place, and white vestments, and incense and flowers. This also is a denial of death, and, much worse, it deprives those in sorrow of the opportunity to grieve and be supported by their loved ones. (I told the friars, "When I die, lay me out in my habit with a purple stole; and if anybody sings 'Alleluia', I'll be back. I'll return in the middle of the night, rattling chains.") Not only is a "happy" funeral celebration an insult to the deceased, but it leaves the real mourners with a great weight of unexpressed grief in their hearts. At death, we all need to struggle with sorrow. This means that we have to deal with death as a reality of life *before* we are suddenly confronted with it.

The Loss of Death

Death has many dark sides to it. First of all, there is our pity for the one who is dying or has died. This is especially true if death is made difficult by reason of a protracted, painful illness or by a sudden horror like an accident or fire. We suffer along with those whom we love and are deeply frustrated that we were not able to do something for them. In our tears, grief, pain, and frustration, we say to God, "What is the use of all of this suffering? Why this innocent person? Why this child?" This is certainly part of what St. Paul calls "the sting of death" (1 Cor 15:56). The powerful model of this suffering is the sorrowful Mother of Christ, shown so movingly in the statue called "The Pietà", an image of pain for one who is loved.

The following poem was written by Coventry Patmore after the death of his little daughter. It expresses in a most moving way the grief that makes someone cry out in anguish to the God whom one loves but who appears to have no mercy.

"IF I WERE DEAD"

"If I were dead you'd sometime say, Poor Child!"
The dear lips quiver'd as they spake,
And the tears break
From eyes, which, not to grieve me, brightly smiled.
Poor Child, poor Child!
I seem to hear your laugh, your talk, your song.
It is not true that Love will do no wrong.
Poor Child!
And did you think, when you so cried and smiled,
How I, in lonely nights, should lie awake,
And of those words your full avengers make?
Poor Child, poor Child!
And now, unless it be
That sweet amends thrice told are come to thee,
O God, have Thou *no* mercy upon me!
Poor Child! [2]

[2] Coventry Patmore, " 'If I Were Dead' ", *Anthology of Catholic Poets*, ed. Joyce Kilmer (Garden City, N.Y.: Doubleday, Image Books, 1955), 197.

The Dark Valley

Another source of grief is the mysterious dark door of death, the shadow of death, the decay of the body, the silence of the grave, the utter lack of response on the part of the dear one who has died, the fact that even among devout believers there are very few known incidents of communication of the dead with this world. While these incidents are not quite as rare as one might suppose, they are rare; and often, when they occur, there is a natural skepticism because of the fact that people often experience what they need to experience, especially when they are in grief. Several sane, educated, down-to-earth people have told me of an experience or clear impression with some gesture of reassurance, coming apparently from a deceased loved one. It would be a mindless prejudice simply to dismiss these reports as the desperate struggle of the mind to console itself. On the other hand, none of these experiences have been something that we could use as a proof for the immortality of the soul. They lack the clarity of the accounts of Christ's Resurrection and are almost never shared by other persons at the time they occur. For the vast majority of the living, death is a dark corridor down which a dear one has passed into silence. Faith remains the only light illumining that corridor, like a searchlight beam pointed down a long tunnel, very dimly revealing the reality at the other end.

Weep for the Living

Perhaps an even greater pain is the loss of the one who has been a support, or even an integral part, of one's life. Obviously, we attend the funerals of many people whom we have known and admired, but we barely saw them—and they were never an integral part of our daily struggle. At any funeral, you can easily distinguish the large group of mourners who have come to pay their respects, and even a debt of gratitude; these are those who deeply experience the loss of this particular person's influence in their lives. For the much smaller group of deeply grieved people, the pain is a pain of loss. It may be a parent grieving for a little child or a child for a parent, a husband for his wife or a very close friend who has been part of someone else's whole life. There are few people who do not experience death as a robber—one who comes with no right and deprives us of what we need, perhaps desperately. It was this deep grief that caused St. Augustine to make the comment, "Weep for the living; don't weep for the dead." It is the painful loss of those we cherish that causes us to think of death as a robbery, because, with no apparent reason, it takes someone we need. We may be angry with God that he has called one whom we needed so very much. With all this in mind, let's try to make some sense of death so that we can know what to do when it comes upon us "like a thief in the night".

The Sting of Death

Several times St. Paul, especially in the Epistle to the Romans, states that death is the result of sin. "Therefore as sin came into the world through one man and death through sin, and so death spread to all men because all men sinned" (Rom 5:12). "For the wages of sin is death, but the free gift of God is eternal life" (Rom 6:23).

A strange teaching, isn't it? Does this mean that if the
world had not fallen, if our first parents had not sinned,
there would be no such thing as death and we would go on
forever and ever in this world? That's an awful idea. Or
does it mean that some great chariot would come down occasionally, and those who were ready to go to the life beyond this one could all get on, and the relatives and friends
could be there to wave them off—something like the tourist
ships of earlier days? The biological processes of life in this
world would eventually take their toll. But in an unfallen
world, everyone would be clearly aware that those who
passed away would go immediately into the Kingdom of
God. It would be a matter for celebration. In such a world,
people would not be so emotionally dependent and consequently would not be wounded by the death of a loved
one. The passing on of a citizen of an unfallen world might
be very much like a graduation. Everybody would know
where he was going and that there was just a bit of a trial to
get there. There might even be tears like those of relatives
on the dock when their parents are leaving on a ten-day
cruise for their fiftieth wedding anniversary.

A Death Celebrated

Even in this fallen world, once in a rare while, you attend
the death of someone who was completely prepared to go.
That's the kind of funeral you could be a bit happy at. I recall the funeral of my dear friend Mother Mary of Jesus of
the Sisters of the Blessed Sacrament in Yonkers. She was
ninety-four years old and had been in the cloister since
1916. I got permission to go into the cloister to visit her
shortly before her death. She was propped up in bed, blind,

lame, and beautifully cared for by her religious sisters. I announced my arrival by asking, "Mother, how are you?" She replied, "Well, Father, you know what Benjamin Franklin used to say." (This lady was filled with surprises. How many cloistered nuns quote Benjamin Franklin?) Cautiously I answered, "Not really." With a twinkle in her blind eyes, she answered with this quotation: "He used to say when he was old, 'I'm still living in the house, but the roof has caved in.'" This was a lady who was ready to go. Would you go to the funeral of someone like this and cry? You might if you missed her as part of your life. But this nun was packed to go. Frequently, devout elderly people are ready to leave this world. The funeral of such a person may not be an occasion of great sorrow. However, if there are those who are deeply dependent on this soul, they will feel the pain of loss despite the age of their dying loved one.

Apart from such rare exceptions of holy souls, I dislike a funeral that's a canonization, especially of people who, with the most kindly of estimates, are going to have a long stay in Purgatory eating Twinkies and drinking room-temperature, bubble-gum-flavored soda. Give me a break! When I go, cry a little bit, please. If you come, cry even if you have to pretend. At least look a little sad. Don't sing "Alleluia", whatever you do. I don't want to be commuting up from Purgatory to haunt people.

Getting Tidied Up for Heaven

This is the place to say something about the much misunderstood and denied doctrine of Purgatory, what the Eastern Orthodox Christians call the place of expiation. Unfortunately, Purgatory has had a very bad press. Many people

grew up with an image of Purgatory as hideous pools of fire
with naked holy souls bobbing up and down like French
fries in a fast-food emporium. The Council of Trent condemned making the temporal punishment in Purgatory
sound hideous. ("The Church gives the name *Purgatory* to
this final purification of the elect, which is entirely different
from the punishment of the damned."[3]) St. Catherine of
Genoa, who wrote a marvelous book on Purgatory, maintained on the basis of her mystical experience that it is a vast
improvement over this life and that the holy souls have no
regrets except that they haven't finally taken their place in
heaven.

> As for paradise, God has placed no doors there. Whoever
> wishes to enter does so. All-merciful God stands there with
> His arms open waiting to receive us into His glory. I also see,
> however, that the divine essence is so pure and light-filled—
> much more than we can imagine—that the soul that has but
> the slightest imperfection would rather throw itself into a
> thousand hells than appear thus before the divine presence.
> Tongue cannot express nor heart understand the full meaning
> of purgatory which the soul willingly accepts as a mercy, the
> realization that that suffering is of no importance compared to
> the removal of the impediment of sin. The greatest suffering of
> the souls in purgatory, it seems to me, is their awareness that
> something in them displeases God, that they have deliberately
> gone against His great goodness. In a state of grace, these souls
> fully grasp the meaning of what blocks them on their way to
> God. This conviction is so strong, from what I have under-
> stood up to this point in life, that by comparison all words,
> sentiments, images, the very idea of justice or truth, seem
> completely false. I am more confused than satisfied with the
> words I have used to express myself, but I have found nothing
> better for what I have felt. All that I have said is as nothing
> compared to what I feel within, the witnessed correspondence

[3] *Catechism of the Catholic Church*, nos. 1030–31.

of love between God and the Soul; for when God sees the Soul pure as it was in its origins, He tugs at it with a glance, draws it and binds it to Himself with a fiery love that by itself could annihilate the immortal soul. In so acting, God so transforms the soul in Him that it knows nothing other than God; and He continues to draw it up unto His fiery love until He restores it to that pure state from which it first issued. As it is being drawn upwards, the soul feels itself melting in the fire of that love of its sweet God, for He will not cease until He has brought the soul to its perfection. That is why the soul seeks to cast off any and all impediments, so that it can be lifted up to God; and such impediments are the cause of the suffering of the souls in purgatory. Not that those souls dwell on their suffering; they dwell rather on the resistance they feel in themselves against the will of God, against His intense and pure love on nothing but drawing them up to Him. And I see rays of lightning darting from that divine love to the creature, so intense and fiery as to annihilate not the body alone but, were it possible, the soul. These rays purify and then annihilate. The soul becomes like gold that becomes purer as it is fired, all dross being cast out.[4]

I'd trade New York for Purgatory any day of the week. It's clearly upscale from Jersey City, where I started out in this life. I'm actually looking forward to it with hope, because I like to travel and visit new places, and I have lots of friends in Purgatory. Once you are there, you are certain of eternal life—which makes it a great deal more pleasant than our scary journey here, which, according to St. Paul, we should follow with fear and trembling.

Protestants have always misunderstood the purpose of Purgatory, even though nowadays you seem to hear them praying for the dead at funerals. (No point in praying for

---

[4] *Catherine of Genoa: Purgation and Purgatory, The Spiritual Dialogue*, ed. Serge Hughes and Benedict J. Groeschel (New York: Paulist Press, 1979), 78–79.

the dead if there's no Purgatory, because the dead would already be in heaven or hell.) The Church has always taught that Christ alone saves us and merits our salvation. We certainly do not do that in Purgatory. And no one ever thought that we did. The most succinct argument I ever heard on Purgatory came from a great old Protestant gentleman, Dr. Samuel Johnson. In one of his many arguments with Boswell he said, in response to a question:

> "What do you think, Sir, of Purgatory, as believed by the Roman Catholicks?" JOHNSON. "Why, Sir, it is a very harmless doctrine. They are of opinion that the generality of mankind are neither so obstinately wicked as to deserve everlasting punishment, nor so good as to merit being admitted into the society of blessed spirits; and therefore that God is graciously pleased to allow a middle state, where they may be purified by certain degrees of suffering. You see, Sir, there is nothing unreasonable in this." BOSWELL. "But then, Sir, their masses for the dead?" JOHNSON. "Why, Sir, if it be once established that there are souls in Purgatory, it is as proper to pray for them, as for our brethren of mankind who are yet in this life." [5]

St. Catherine of Genoa, being a mystic and not a *littérateur* like Dr. Johnson, gave us a more profound insight. For her, Purgatory is a gift of God's mercy permitting us to cooperate with his grace in removing all the obstacles that we put between ourselves and his love. In the following lines from her book, Catherine gives the lie to those dismal images which seem to contradict the very words of Scripture that "the souls of the just are in the hands of God" (Wis 3:1).

> I see the sufferings of the souls in purgatory are endurable because of two considerations. The first is the willingness to suf-

[5] James Boswell, *The Life of Samuel Johnson* (New York: The Modern Library, 1950), 356.

fer, the certainty that God has been most merciful to them in the light of what they deserved and of what God offers them. If God's mercy did not temper His justice—that justice which has been satisfied with the blood of Jesus Christ—one sin alone would deserve a thousand eternal hells. Knowing, therefore, that they suffer justly, those souls accept the ordinance of God and would not think of doing otherwise. The other considera-tion that sustains those souls is a certain joy that is never want-ing and that, indeed, increases as they come closer to God. Their rejoicing is for God's ordinance, His love and mercy, into which each soul sees according to his capacity. These in-sights are not of the souls' own doing. They are seen in God, in whom they are more absorbed than in their own suffering, for the briefest vision of God far surpasses any human joy or suffering.[6]

We can hardly paint a horrible picture of Purgatory and still say that the dead who are on their spiritual journey to-ward their heavenly reality are safely in the hands of God. An interesting event took place in the life of the foundress of the Sisters of the Cenacle, St. Marie Thérèse Couderc. Just a few days before her death, her ears were filled with beautiful celestial choral singing. She described it thus:

"I do not know what is happening. . . . One might think that illness has robbed me of my right senses. Since yesterday, I have been surrounded by a multitude who unceasingly pray and pray, in penetrating tones, and a reverence beyond any-thing I have ever known. They chant also in solemn tone hymns, psalms, and liturgical prayers. They supplicate, they moan with pain, they adore the Divine Majesty. They praise that Majesty with a unity, a harmony, a faith, a hope, a love in-effable. I believe they are the souls in Purgatory. For hours at a time I am thus taken up in them, for in spite of myself I am forced to join them. At times I am affrighted, for they envelop me, they draw very close to me. They are suffering and they

[6] *Catherine of Genoa*, 84.

show it in a heart-rending way. I would indeed be delivered from this: I have asked Our Lord to deliver me. but He does not hear me." [7]

When the Mother General was told this by the dying saint, she advised her to speak to her confessor about the singing. The Mother General writes:

> When I visited her again, all smiles, she looked at me and said: "The Father told me not to fear. He believes that these are the souls in Purgatory. Since they are friends of God, because they love Him and are beloved by Him, they are in His Eyes a blessed society. I have not slept this night. They have not left me. I have seen among them some of our own. I have seen many priests and religious. When this morning I had received the Sacred Host, they intoned the *Te Deum*. At the fourth verse, in spite of every effort I made to be attentive as usual to Our Lord, I was forced to follow them and to sing with them: Holy, Holy, Holy, Lord God of Sabaoth.
>
> "It was most wonderful. I would have to live a very long time before I could forget that harmony, those accents, that reverence of which nothing on earth can give even a suggestion. Every verse was sung with a feeling suited to the praise or the appeal which it expressed. When they came to the last verse—In thee, O Lord, have I hoped: let me never be confounded—they sang it at least ten times, with a humility and ardor, a confidence overflowing with love. They are there all the time. I cannot understand why they are not heard. Don't you hear them now?"
>
> Again she said to me: "They are a multitude. Among them are the voices of men, the voices of women, the voices of children. . . . Oh, how they pray: how they sing! Oh, if we could pray as they do! How rough, how unbecoming in comparison is our way of praying! Where, indeed, is our reverence?" [8]

---

[7] Henry Perroy, *A Great and Humble Soul: Mother Thérèse Couderc, Foundress of the Society of Our Lady of the Retreat in the Cenacle (1805–1885)*, trans. John J. Burke (New York: Paulist Press, 1933), 220–21.

[8] Ibid., 221.

If one thinks about death, it's helpful to think about what comes after it. It stands to reason, as Dr. Johnson pointed out, that most of us will be headed toward Purgatory, so it's not a bad idea to spend a little time thinking about that wonderful preparation for our final entrance into the Kingdom of God. If you happen to be a canonizable saint, it's not necessary to do this, but otherwise I think it is time well spent.

Death Is Awesome

Despite the reassurances that faith gives us and that our Divine Savior gave to the apostles, death remains an awesome event. It's frightening. I have dear friends here in New York, the Dominican Sisters of Hawthorne, who literally live with death. Their community takes care only of people who are dying of cancer, especially poor people who can't pay. Think of it. If you teach school, your students are going to live on after you go, and, you hope, some of them will remember something you taught. For these sisters, the final success in their apostolate is to see a person die a peaceful and even holy death. This is a marvelous vocation, but extremely challenging because, even for these sisters, death is a robber of the people they have come to know and work with. However, if one visits one of their several homes for the dying, one would not come away with a terrible fear of death. The sisters constantly have to face the same questions that you and I face: Why? Why does a young mother die of cancer? Why does a good person who has lived a helpful life need to die so painfully?

This leads all of us to the awesome questions of death. Death frequently comes in a terrible way, utterly unforeseen and to those who are completely innocent. When I was first writing this series, a truck driver delivering a huge tank of gasoline went into a railroad crossing and found a traffic jam in front of him. Suddenly the bell began to ring, warning him that a train was coming. He couldn't get the truck off the tracks fast enough. He tried to back up, but the gates came down on top of his truck. The engineer saw him and threw the engines into reverse, but the train could not be stopped that quickly and hit the gasoline truck at forty-five miles an hour. The driver was burned to death along with five other people waiting at the crossing. One elderly man was blown out of his car and found himself running down the street, his clothes aflame; but his dear wife never got out of the car. Why? I don't know.

Death confronts us with the mysterious element in life. In contemporary society, we deny the existence of the mysterious. Many things are mysterious—life, love, darkness—but what is more mysterious than eternity? If you can't cope with mystery, this life is going to drive you mad or make you cynical or terribly depressed. Life is filled with many unanswered questions. To be honest, if we did not seek answers to these questions, we'd all be sheep. Mystery gives suffering humanity its greatest dignity. Death brings us directly into an unavoidable confrontation with the mysteriousness of life. This is true whether death is expected or sudden, whether it is the welcomed death of a very ill person who longs to go home or whether it is seen as the worst possible thing—the sickness of a small child or a person who has life in front of him. When death arrives it is usually as a mystery. But what do we do in the case of this mystery? People of every religion and people in the world, every racial group, every culture—what do they do when death comes? They pray. Even unbelievers pray. They may never pray at any other time, but they pray in the presence of death, because death is what gives life some dimensions, its mystery and its meaning. Death is the frame around life. As we make our way through life we need to learn the lessons that death can teach us. For the Christian, the approach of death has a great message: Jesus Christ identified himself with us to such an extent that he was willing not only to die, but to endure a terrible and painful death.

The Death of a Star

I discovered a beautiful statement that brings out the meaning of death in, of all places, the sports section of the *New York Times*. Arthur Ashe, the tennis star who contracted AIDS through a blood transfusion, in an article written after his death, was reported to have said to the students of a community college during his terminal period:

> I've had a religious faith, growing up in the South and black and having the church as the focal point of your life. . . . And I was reminded of something Jesus said on the cross, "My God, my God, why hast thou forsaken me?" Remember, Jesus was poor, humble and of a despised minority. . . . And Jesus asked the question, in effect, why must the innocent suffer. I'm not so innocent, I mean I'm hardly a perfect human being. But you ask yourself about it, "Why me?" and then I think, "Why not me?"
>
> Why should I be spared what some others have been afflicted with? And I have to think of all the good things in my life: of having a great wife and daughter and family and friends, of winning at Wimbledon and the U.S. Open, and playing for and coaching the Davis Cup team, getting a free scholarship to UCLA—all kinds of good things. You could ask about this, "Why me?" Sometimes there are no explanations for things, especially things that are bad.[9]

---

[9] "The Changing Faces of Arthur Ashe: From Private Pain to Public Service", *New York Times*, Sunday Sports Section, Oct. 25, 1992.

Arthur Ashe was not a religious leader, but he was a man of faith. I'm so grateful that a lay person and a very respected star spoke to the very issue that, for the Christian, death must focus on—the fact that the Son of God came here and did not die a comfortable death, surrounded by holy disciples like St. Francis or Gautama Buddha or even Father Damien and his beloved lepers. Saints often had beautiful deaths surrounded by followers singing and praying to the Lord. But Jesus died surrounded by his enemies and endured for us the most difficult death. This was a consoling truth for Arthur Ashe, and it can be for you too.

Death Is Not Forever

As you consider the death of those dear to you, keep in mind that death does not rob us forever. It does rob us now of someone we love and need very much. We can be very angry at death and at a God who allows it to rob us. Recall that God himself came and took up the heavy burden of a painful, miserable, horrible death by torture. While we complain, we know that he has suffered this before us. It does not answer all the questions, but the Cross does put them in perspective.

Learning from Death

Death is a powerful teacher and has many lessons to teach us. Learn from death that nothing in this world lasts forever, that everything in this life passes away. Learn from death not to cling to anything in such a way that you can't go on without it. Instead, learn to refer all things to eternity. Do not be so comfortable with anything in this world that you will be unprepared to leave it. Faith gives us the immense consolation of knowing that we shall have restored to us on the other side of the grave all the good things we had in this world but in a transcendingly beautiful way. Naturally we're frightened. We don't know what death is like. "Eye has not seen, ear has not heard, it has not entered our hearts to think" (1 Cor 2:9). But we do know, Christ tells us, "In my Father's house there are many mansions" (Jn 14:2).

I am so anxious for believers and seekers to know about this that I have prayed for a long terminal illness myself. I hope that the Lord will give me time to record some reflections on the Christian attitude toward death while I'm dying. Such talks should be rather convincing. I've spoken to the Daughters of St. Paul, who make video tapes, and the Hawthorne Dominicans, who care for the dying—and maybe we can cut a deal. They'll bring in the cameras, and I'll be propped up in the Rosary Hill Home. We'll see if I'm as sassy then as I am now. I would just as soon get cancer if I'm going to get anything, so I can go to Rosary Hill. I want to give the message, "Don't run away from death. Don't fight death. And when death is stealing someone close to you, for heaven's sake, pray. Pray long, pray well, pray even desperately, pray from the depths of your heart. It is so pathetic to go to funerals and not see anyone praying."

Grief Done Well

When St. Monica was dying, her two sons, Augustine and Navigius, said something to this effect, "Mother, hold on. We'll take a ship and get you back to Africa so you can be buried in your native soil." Monica was not interested in funerals—she was interested in prayers and especially in having the sacrifice of Christ's Body and Blood offered for her soul. Augustine recalls:

> As death was approaching soon my mother was not concerned that her body be elegantly dressed or embalmed with no thought of choosing a monument or being buried at home. She made no request but only expressed her wish that she be remembered at your altar. She attended [Mass] without missing a day when she knew that the Holy Victim is offered who blots out the handwriting of the decree against us and who defeats the enemy who seeks to condemn us by collecting our sins but who found nothing in him in whom we are conquerors. . . . To this sacrament of our redemption your handmaid was bound in her soul by the bond of faith. Let no one take her away from your protection. Let the evil beast not stand in her way by force or deceit. She will never claim that she owes nothing lest that accuser contradict her, but she will proclaim that her debts have been remitted by him to whom no one can return the ransom although he owed nothing himself. So let her rest in peace, together with her husband for she had no other husband but served him in patience, bringing forth fruit for you and winning him to your cause. And inspire, O my Lord, my God, your servants my brothers whom I serve with heart and voice and pen that as many of them as read this statement may remember at your altar the servant Monica with Patritius her husband by whose bodies you brought me into this life though I know not how. May they with loving mind remember my parents in this transitory life, my brothers who serve you as our Father in our Catholic mother and who are to be my fellow citizens in the eternal Jerusalem which your people yearn for in their pilgrimage from birth until they finally arrive there.[10]

What more loving and beneficial thing can one do for the dead than to offer the Sacrifice of Christ for them. How

---

[10] St. Augustine, *Confessions*, book IX, chap. 13 (translation by the author).

beautiful and consoling to pray for the dead on their journey. We have no idea what that journey is like. If they're already saints in the wonderful mystical reality of heaven, then let's pray with them. The saints live in the celebration of the Paschal Mystery of which the Liturgy of the Mass in this world is the only substantial reflection. At the Liturgy they attend, Christ is the High Priest. Here in this world, we poor men who are called priests stand in for him according to his command.

Make up your mind to use death as we are supposed to. It can lift our eyes to eternity. And when it's a painful death, a death that may make you angry, that seems unjust and unfair—for example, an innocent person killed by malice—it is most important to pray. Then we need to remind ourselves that this innocent one has walked down a very short corridor into the light of God. However painful their dying may be, no matter how racked their bodies are with pain, the dying pass along a very short corridor. If they are prepared, they enter immediately into eternal life. We pray for loved ones on their journey that they may already be at peace with God. And we are even told by Blessed Sister Faustina, the mystic of Divine Mercy, that she believed that Christ had told her that he dialogues with the soul on the way to perdition. She records that it was revealed to her that when no human voice can speak to the dying person, Christ himself comes and calls to that soul.[11] I believe this. Christ did not die on the Cross, he did not endure what he endured in life, for people to be lost. If I were on my way to being lost [and St. Paul says we should "work out" our salvation "with fear and trembling" (Phil 2:12)], could I look into the merciful eyes

---

[11] Rev. George Kosicki, C.S.B., *Now Is the Time for Mercy* (Steubenville, Ohio: Franciscan University Press, 1991), 8–11.

of Christ and say, "No"? The answer is I can't save myself, but I must give my consent to my salvation. How God calls forth this consent is something very mysterious. We should be hopeful for those who led sinful lives. Don't be jealous of them. We who believe have received so much more than they did. Many apparently did not receive very much. Maybe they were rich, maybe their lives were full of pleasure, but it was a hollow bubble. You and I are really the rich people. If we have faith and the sacraments, we are really rich with a wealth that does not perish.

St. John of the Cross teaches that the sun, the moon, the stars, the earth, the sea, time, eternity, and the Mother of God all belong to us. We can't be poor. We can't be completely unfortunate. We have the angels and the saints for friends. Who owns the earth? Our heavenly Father. We are not poor. Worldly, unbelieving, grasping, manipulative people—they are the poor ones. They've invested their lives in junk. Invest your life in eternity if you are a believer. Note that those who are wealthy and are real believers act the same way as the other believers do. They are generous with what they have. They keep before their eyes very clearly that they will take with them only what they have given away.

Death Comes to All

This chapter has been about the grief we experience when death robs us of those we love and need, but ultimately death comes to each of us. If you want, you can see it not as a robber but as a deliverance. Death comes to all. It is their shepherd, and yours and mine as well. In this we must have hope. Christ shows us that the poorest of the poor can be saved. He saves a thief as he himself is dying on the Cross. That fact alone should give us great hope. One reader's brother was a crook. Another person's uncle was a schemer. Someone else in your family was a drunk. Don't give up hope. Remember the good thief; he was hanging on the cross when he was saved. Blessed Angela of Folingno, the Franciscan mystic, writes that she believed that there are those who appear to men to be lost in hell who were raised into heaven.

What about your death, my death? It's scary. We've never been there before. The physical effects of dying are disastrous. I once took a little boy from Children's Village to the funeral of his brother, who had been killed. He asked me, "When he's there in the casket will he be able to talk to me?" It was so sad that I had to explain to him that his brother could not speak.

Not long ago I conducted a funeral in Harlem for an elderly lady named Vivian. She was a devout, kindly, gentle woman and belonged to some little storefront church. In her old age she was really too ill to go out. Her family was on our list for food baskets, and so they called me to do the funeral service. I walked up to the funeral parlor with her husband, a dignified and friendly gentleman. I never knew the first names of either of these people because I always called them "Grandma" and "Grandpa". They were quite on in years for *me* to use this designation. "Grandpa" and I went into the funeral parlor together, and we paused at the side of the casket. "She was the finest woman in the world . . . the finest woman in the world." He kept saying that. At the end of the brief service, I got them to pray for "Grandma" on her journey. They thought it was a sensible thing to do. "Grandpa" came up to the casket before we left. So simply and directly he stood there with his hands on the casket and said over and over again, "I love you." It was beautiful and solemn. Don't forget this: someday it will be your funeral. Make sure you live in such a way that it will be both sorrowful and beautiful for those you leave behind.

Recently a man walked up to me after a conference and whispered, "My wife doesn't know this, but I'm dying of cancer." I replied, "I'm dying of life, so let's pray for each other." We've all got a terminal illness. It's called life.

Death looms before us like a great door. It is awesome because it is larger than any other reality we ever face. It sums up all that has been and brings to an end all that might be yet to happen. It is a great and silent door. But for the person of faith, it becomes an inviting mystery. In the course of the years one becomes weary of conflict and sorrow. One longs for the fulfillment of the most profound needs of the human heart—for peace from conflict within and without, for a place free of danger and disappointment, for relationships untroubled by change and unmarred by selfishness. One longs to see, at last, the beauty of God, which has summoned us throughout life, shining out here and there. The words of the Psalm take on a poignant meaning as one gets older, "I have loved, O Lord, the beauty of thy house and the place where thy glory dwells" (Ps 26:8). One desires to embrace again loved ones gone long ago—from childhood and adolescence. Death becomes a possibility of going home to our Father's house. For the believer, it begins to lose the bitterness and sting that St. Paul spoke about and begins faintly to resemble what death was supposed to be before the Fall, a passing on to a far better place, a coming home after a long journey.

Cardinal Newman, who lived into his nineties, often wrote about death. In this prayer, which is called "God the Sole Stay for Eternity", he teaches us a great deal about God and eternity.

Thou, O my God, art ever new, though Thou art also most ancient—Thou alone art the food for eternity. I am to live forever, not for a time—and I have no power over my own being; I cannot destroy myself, even though I were so wicked as to wish to do so. I must live on, with intellect and consciousness for ever, in spite of myself. Without Thee eternity would be another name for eternal misery. In Thee alone have I that which can stay me up for ever: Thou alone art the food of my soul. Thou alone art inexhaustible, and ever offerest to me something new to know, something new to love. At the end of millions of years I shall know Thee so little, that I shall seem to myself only beginning. At the end of millions of years I shall find in Thee the same, or rather, greater sweetness than at first, and shall seem then only to be beginning to enjoy Thee: and so on for eternity I shall ever be a little child beginning to be taught the rudiments of Thy infinite Divine Nature. For Thou art Thyself the seat and centre of all that is good, and the only substance in this universe of shadows, and the heaven in which blessed spirits live and rejoice.

My God, I take Thee for my portion. From mere prudence I turn away from the world to Thee; I give up the world for Thee. I renounce that which it promises for Him who performs. To whom else should I go? I desire to find and feed on Thee here; I desire to feed on Thee, Jesu, my Lord, who are risen, who hast gone up on high, who yet remainest with Thy people on earth. I look up to Thee; I look for the Living Bread which is in heaven; which comes down from heaven. Give me ever of this Bread. Destroy this life, which will soon perish— even though Thou dost not destroy it, and fill me with that supernatural life which will never die.[12]

This is something to think about when you go to a funeral. You look at the body and you say, "Where is your soul?" Perhaps the deceased has entered, like the saints, immediately into his place forever—remember, one must be

---

[12] John Henry Newman, Meditations on Christian Doctrine, XXIII, *Prayers, Verses, and Devotions* (San Francisco: Ignatius Press, 1989), 443–44.

completely innocent and utterly pure to go to that place of absolute innocence and purity. That's why, if you're planning on missing Purgatory, you may be in for a disappointment. We do strive to accept salvation completely while we are on earth, but most of us have never opened our hearts completely to it. This is what happens in Purgatory. God doesn't change while we're in Purgatory. We change.

What's It Like?

There are some, and may they be very few and may they be no one who is dear to us, who do not go into eternal life. It is really too terrible to write about. It is so terrible a truth that Christ died in order that we would be delivered from hell. I would rather turn my attention to our eternal goal. Frank Sheed used to say to me, "I've heard a dozen good sermons on hell, but I've never heard a good sermon on heaven." And Lord knows, I couldn't preach one. That great old Catholic apologist used to say: "All the preachers seem to be able to do is come up with an eternal church service which is not very appealing. (I've been to church services I thought were going to be eternal.) You can imagine an infinite number of altar boys carrying incense in a procession or the Mormon Tabernacle Choir on an endless tape. None of this is terribly appealing." What is heaven like? I can't tell you, but we do have a hint and it's right in the Bible. These words are, regrettably, unfamiliar to people. I was recently present at the death of a man who died from AIDS but who had been a very active Charismatic. He was a very devout man after he returned to the Church and still didn't know he had AIDS from his earlier life. He was well prepared. When I read those words, there were several Charismatics present, and none of them seemed to know where the words were in the Bible. Even the evangelical Protestants who were present seemed to be equally unfamiliar with the words. I was amazed. I read them often. They are from the very last pages of the Bible. They tell us something about what it's like in the Kingdom of God.

> Then I saw a great white throne and him who sat upon it; from his presence earth and sky fled away, and no place was found for them. And I saw the dead, great and small, standing before the throne, and books were opened. Also another book was opened, which is the book of life. And the dead were judged by what was written in the books, by what they had done. And the sea gave up the dead in it, Death and Hades gave up the dead in them, and all were judged by what they had done. Then Death and Hades were thrown into the lake of fire. This is the second death, the lake of fire; and if any one's name was not found written in the book of life, he was thrown into the lake of fire.
>
> Then I saw a new heaven and a new earth; for the first heaven and the first earth had passed away, and the sea was no more. And I saw the holy city, new Jerusalem, coming down out of heaven from God, prepared as a bride adorned for her husband; and I heard a great voice from the throne saying, "Behold, the dwelling of God is with men. He will dwell with them, and they shall be his people, and God himself will be with them; he will wipe away every tear from their eyes, and death shall be no more, neither shall there be mourning nor crying nor pain any more, for the former things have passed away." And he who sat upon the throne said, "Behold I make all things new." Also he said, "Write this, for these words are trustworthy and true." And he said to me, "It is done! I am the Alpha and the Omega, the beginning and the end. To the thirsty I will give water without price from the fountain of the water of life. He who conquers shall have this heritage, and I will be his God and he shall be my son" (Rev 20:11–21; 21:1–7).

I believe this! I utterly, absolutely believe it, although the words themselves, because they are human words, are incapable of communicating or containing the whole reality. But when life makes no sense, when things seem utterly impossible, when all is lost and I experience one of those many little deaths that get us all ready for the great death, when that happens, I think of these words. And I say: "I know that my Redeemer lives and that in the last day I shall rise out of the earth" (Job 19:25). Amen.

— *Prayer* —

O HOLY SPIRIT, enlighten my mind that death may not be my enemy, that I may not fear it in an unseemly way for a Christian, that I may not run from death, so that when death comes and takes those dear to me, I may welcome their release from this valley of tears although I am myself deeply moved and even deprived by their departure from this world. Let me know that death reminds each of us of the infinite reality of life with you. Let me see all things in the perspective of death and everlasting life. And let me not be filled with grief either at the anticipation of my own death or the experience of the death of those dear to me. Rather, strengthen my faith, that in the midst of this changing world I may always come closer to you, who never change and who await me and those dear to me together with the Father and the Son in life everlasting. Amen.

What Do We Do
When Everything Falls Apart?

What do we do when everything falls apart? This happens in most people's lives at least once. We all experience a month or a year or a time when nothing at all makes sense. Things we have worked hardest to accomplish, to provide for others, are destroyed overnight.

It may appear that some people are spared this experience. They seem to live lives where everything fits together, everything makes sense, everything is pleasant if not wonderful. But, as we have seen, this is an illusion because it isn't true in anyone's life. It is part of old English manners that define our customs not to share one's griefs or sorrows with others. So we all live with the illusion that everyone else is having a wonderful time. Ask others how they're doing, and they'll say, "Fine." And they'll ask you, and you will say, "Fine." None of us is doing fine at all. It's a blessing to work with the poor—they don't say, "Fine." Ask them how things are going, and they'll say, "Awful."

It often happens that those who have done the best they could in life find themselves ruined by a business collapse, by a failure in their family—perhaps a marriage that they entered into, giving their all for a lifetime, just falls apart, or someone they trusted fails them completely. People have entered into religious life only to see the community that they served fall apart. One lives surrounded by people who have been punished by life in a way that makes no sense at all. Perhaps there is that rare person (statistically this may happen) whose life goes marvelously and who finally has a nice retirement. But then he too will die. It's all going to fall apart, isn't it. Those of us who have had tough times in life say, "Oh, just another death: mine." We're prepared for it. But someone for whom life has been gentle and placid (and there are very, very few such) is going to be so shocked, so appalled that he won't quite know what to do. In the notes of Cardinal Cooke I found a little line that read, "The man who has suffered will not fear death."

A Time to Believe

When things fall apart and all seems to be ruined and when the terrible question "What do you do when nothing makes sense?" comes right home, the answer is that it is the time to believe. It is the time for faith. In the strongest possible New Testament sense of that word, one must believe. One must grab onto God. It's nothing abstract like: "I think there must be a God because there are such beautiful trees and stars. Where did this all come from?" No, it's nothing like that. It's powerful. It's burning. "God, you are there, and I have nothing else to cling to." One must be able to say, "I believe that God's goodness is going to bring about some greater good by this horror. It may not be a great good for me in this world, but it will be a great good some-place, somewhere, perhaps for those I love in the next world."

My principal work in life brings me into contact with a number of people whose lives have come down in flames. I expected to work as a priest-psychologist with young delinquents. Oh, for those easy days again! I had to deal with simple problems like kids stealing cars and robbing banks. I was also a spiritual director working with nice, pleasant problems like scrupulosity and people experiencing aridity in prayer or priest assistants who didn't get along with their pastors. These are easy problems. In recent years, with the media attack on the Church and with the mysterious phenomena of sexual abuse and other forms of moral disaster, my life as a psychologist has become extraordinarily challenged. Recently, I was with a group of psychologists, many of them in practice longer than I have been. We all agreed that a decade ago you could work five years as a psychologist and never hear anyone speak about sexual abuse. Now we hear about it everywhere. The estimate is that one tenth of adult women in the United States can remember some experience of abuse in childhood, from a relative or a neighbor or a friend. Therapists ask, "How come no one ever talked about this before?" I went ten years before I ever met anyone who mentioned sexual abuse to me.

An area that I was rather unaware of was the sexual failure of some clergy—failure to observe celibacy. I became aware that many priests wanted dispensations to marry, but then all of a sudden I heard about sexual misbehavior with teenagers. Most of the time this horrified the person responsible when it occurred. They were usually devastated even when no one else ever knew what happened. And the most distressing experience of all was to work with the victims. What can one say to assuage their pain?

It was in the crucible of such suffering and disaster that I began to think of the experiences that so many have of their lives falling apart. Be it terminal illness or the death of a dear one or personal tragedy, even if we can't answer the question "Why?", we must move on to ask "What?" There must be something one can do to help.

Divine Providence

Whatever the occasion for people coming to me when their lives are in ruins, I always turn to one of my cherished books, *Abandonment to Divine Providence*, by Jean-Pierre de Caussade, S.J.[1]

I strongly suggest that you get this work and meditate on it if you are in any desperate situation. Père de Caussade (d. 1751) wrote a series of talks to cloistered nuns on the topic of total trust in God during the upheavals and moral scandals of eighteenth-century France. These and his spiritual letters have been published. I am one out of many hundreds of thousands who have benefited immeasurably over the years from his conferences and letters. His teaching is summed up in the following sample taken from a letter to a nun.

> I am experiencing here the constant care of divine Providence, for no sooner have I sacrificed everything to God than he discovers a remedy for everything and causes me to find whatever I need. When I find myself without resource, I place all my affairs in the hands of Providence, I hope everything from it, I have recourse to it in everything and for everything; I thank God ceaselessly for everything, receiving everything from his divine hand. And never does he fail us, so long as we put all our confidence in his protection. But what do people do as a rule? They try to substitute their own blind and impotent providence for the infinitely wise and good providence of God;

[1] Jean-Pierre de Caussade, S.J., *Abandonment to Divine Providence*, trans. John Beevers (New York: Doubleday, 1975). Other translations are available also.

they base themselves on their own efforts, and by doing so they place themselves outside the order of divine love and lose all the support they would have had in carrying out that order. What folly! How can we doubt that God understands our interests much better than we do and that his dispositions of events in regard to us are advantageous even when we do not understand them? Would not a little wisdom be enough to determine us to allow ourselves to be led with docility by his Providence, though we cannot understand all the secret springs which God brings into play, or the particular ends that he has in mind? [2]

In your life, when things begin to fall apart, apparently by happenstance, perhaps because of the ill will of others, or on the occasion of terminal illness or death or economic insecurity or the loss of a position—when things start to fall apart, for heaven's sake, take yourself to prayer. Not prayer that is going to help you tell God what to do. That's not very helpful prayer. God already knows what to do. But prayer that will reassure you that you are in the hands of God.

One Holy Week, I heard confessions in Riker's Island, the penitentiary for New York City. I was in what is called the Bing—the section for people who flunked out of maximum security. The inmates are in their cells twenty-three hours a day. No radio, no nothing, just a cell. Most of these poor fellows were on their way to the Bing before they set foot on earth. Almost all come from the most difficult circumstances, and yet some know how to pray. I admit that their prayers sound like they are talking God into something. They pray like crooks because that's how they do everything. Many are doing life sentences on the installment plan—five years now, ten years later. My sermon was very simple: "Keep your eyes open, your mouth shut, your hands in your pockets, and walk, do not run, away from police cars; and pray." Somehow, mysteriously, even these desperate men know how to pray. You know how to pray. We all really have it within us to pray. I don't mean the nice prayers or meditations, but the prayers of desperate faith. You, I, everyone knows how to pray in the dark time.

One of my favorite spiritual writers, Blessed Julian of Norwich, sums this thought up beautifully:

> When the soul is tempest tossed, troubled and cut off by worries, then is the time to pray. In such a way as to make the soul willing and responsive toward God. But there is no kind of prayer that can make God more responsive to the soul for God is always constantly responsive. And so I saw that whenever we feel the need to pray, the Good Lord follows us helping our desire. And when by His special grace, we behold Him clearly, knowing no other need, then we follow Him and He draws us to Himself by love. I saw this—that it is God's great unceasing work in everything, that it happens, that it is done well, that His work is done so wisely and mightily that it is beyond our power to imagine or guess or think.[3]

I remember one man I was working with who, in a devastating situation, mentioned the position he was in when he resigned. A deeply penitent and prayerful man, he said, "Better to lose that position than to lose your soul." It is important to do what that man did when one's life falls apart. It is very important to believe that even in the most dreadful circumstances God is working toward our salvation. By prayer, by good works, by a life of dedication, by carrying the cross, one may give God the chance to bring good out of evil. It is only by a misuse of the mysterious power of the human will that we can stop God from bring-

---

[3] *Daily Readings with Julian of Norwich*, ed. Robert Llewelyn, trans. Sheila Upjohn (Springfield, Ill.: Templegate, 1985), chap. 43, showing 14.

ing good out of evil. Isn't that what the Passion and death of Jesus Christ tell us?

We are all concerned about the Church in these times. Believe me, it has been worse. The worst day for the Catholic Church was the first Holy Thursday. On that day Judas Iscariot betrayed Jesus for thirty pieces of silver. The other apostles ran away. Only the holy women, starting with our Lady, stayed faithful to Christ. What did they do? They stood in prayerful vigil around him. They appeared to be helpless, but they were faithful. They believed.

How Unsearchable His Ways

Let me share with you an event that demonstrates how God is there in the worst of times. I'm going to use this man's story as an example because he was disgraced in public on television. This priest was known for being very kind, responsive, and helpful, doing deeds of extraordinary kindness, going out of his way, extending himself. It happened in a lonely country parish that a woman who had been previously married took a shine to him and repeatedly insisted, with threats of suicide, that he marry her. This priest did not know how to say "No." He was driven to the verge of a mental breakdown. He arrived at my doorstep in a state of extreme emotional exhaustion and fatigue. He had married this woman before a justice of the peace a few days before without even notifying anyone that he was leaving the priesthood, because the day before this happened he had no intention of departing. It appeared that he was automatically dismissed from the priesthood, suspended from all ecclesiastical functions, and dismissed from his religious order. He had stayed with this woman only one day. He left and went immediately to a friend, who called and asked me to help him. I spoke to some canon lawyers, pointing out that the whole thing had happened under duress. The marriage was invalid morally, canonically, and probably even civilly. The apparent marriage was done under extreme psychological duress. He had absolutely no intention of returning to that woman. I don't think he had any intention of staying with her in the first place, but he was afraid she would carry out her suicide threats.

He made a retreat with us. Because the marriage was so doubtful, on the advice of a couple of canonists I acceded to his request to concelebrate Mass during the retreat. I had scruples about allowing this, but as you will see it was the right thing to do. On the last day of the retreat, I spoke to the priests about the last things—judgment, hell, and heaven. (I'm not known as a "Doctor Feelgood" type.) I spoke about life and death. The day before, this man had sat all day in chapel and cried. His years as a priest, at least as an active priest, were probably over. When I came back in the afternoon from teaching, an ambulance was pulling away from the retreat house. The pressure of this entire thing had brought him to death. He had suffered a fatal heart attack, surviving just long enough for another priest to give him the holy anointing. Literally, his life had not only been ruined; it had been destroyed. He had prayed desperately with many tears of repentance. In his mysterious ways, God had delivered him from what the Church may not have been able to deliver him. There are worse things than death.

Right this minute, some readers are struggling with extraordinarily heavy burdens, as a consequence of mistakes they made, mistakes that may have appeared very small in the eyes of God. There is an old Irish expression, "in the eyes of God". "They're not married in the eyes of God. . . . It's not right in the eyes of God." Who knows what is in the eyes of God? I would never pretend to see anything with the divine eyes. The eyes of the Church are something else, like bifocals. We poor slobs who are left the duty of taking on the mission of the apostles—bishops, priests, and deacons—we can't see things with the eyes of God. Once, when I was chairing a meeting, I said, "You know, I'm not at all sure what we should do in this case." Someone looked up and remarked that our Lord was always sure what he was supposed to do. I replied that our Lord walked on the sea, turned water into wine, and rose from the dead. I'm like the Church: I dotter along the way. We're all plodding along.

In your own life, dark times will come. If they are very dark and bitter, know that you have plenty of company. Suppose an angel appeared to me and said, "Benedict, you've had enough trouble already and so you're going to lead a charmed life from now on, like in the movie *The Sound of Music*. From now on everything will be happy and easy. It won't turn to gold, but it will be quite livable. No more big troubles between now and your fatal heart attack. Everything will be lovely! Will you accept that?" I would say, "No. Deliver me, O God." I wouldn't accept it for one minute. I'd get the holy water and sprinkle it on the angel, shouting, "You're from the devil. Get out of here. Take off." I would not want to be separated from the sufferings and sorrows of everyone else. I would absolutely reject such a chocolate-covered horror. The Lord has already heard my prayer, because actually, when you're a priest, you hardly even have time for your own troubles. I can't fit them in. I look forward to the day I put this message on my phone answering machine: "This is Father Benedict.

Don't call back, because I just died. I hope I'll be praying for you in Purgatory."

The Martyrs—Witnesses to Good Out of Evil

What is more distressing to us than the death of the innocent? Whether it is a Christian in ancient Rome or the Jews in Auschwitz or the bomb victims of London or Hiroshima—regardless of who caused it or why, the death of the innocent is the ultimate abomination. And people are so casual about this. Starvation, abortion, political machinations—all these cry out that something is terribly wrong. This is especially true when the victim is a child—a St. Maria Goretti or an Anne Frank.

One group of victims, the martyrs, proclaim the message that all believers must hold onto in the worst situations. We often think of them as witnesses to the faith, and indeed they do give a powerful testimony to life after death. But they also remind us that God brings good out of evil. Innumerable innocent people have died because they were in the way and seemed expendable or because of the greed and sinfulness of man. The martyrs thought that the loss of life was not the ultimate disaster. We need to listen to them in order to put our experience of life into perspective. The martyrs remind us that God continues to bring immense good out of evil. We have been horrified by dreadful crimes against generous apostles in recent years—for instance, in Central America, the assassination of Archbishop Romero, the killing of the Jesuit priests, and the murder of sisters, one of whom, a Maryknoll sister, I had taught. There have been so many in this century. These were horrible, dreadful, bloodthirsty, hideous events. But out of these things, which were only permitted by God and perpetrated by the free will of human beings, he can bring immense good. As Scripture says, "Their blood cries out."

As one distressed and horrified by the abortion holocaust in our country, I am forced to believe that out of this terrible thing God will bring some good. I can't tell how. I had a rabbi friend who lost his family to the Nazis in Auschwitz, and he used to say to me, "I don't understand this, but the Almighty will bring some good out of it."

A Senseless Deed

I have decided to bring this book to an end with a description of a senseless murder by a government. It's something that makes no sense. One of the more peculiar things in modern times has been the persecution of the Catholic Church and religion in general in Mexico. The Republic of Mexico was founded by a Catholic priest, Father Hidalgo. He is their George Washington. Mexico in many ways was settled and brought into the modern world by the Church. The largest number of people ever converted in a single event was the conversion of the Aztecs by the apparition of Our Lady of Guadalupe. In a period of twenty years, eight million people entered the Church. But somehow the government of Mexico, a land that is 95 percent Catholic, for a hundred years perpetrated the most vicious and cruel persecution of the Catholic Church, abetted, I'm sorry to tell you, by the American government. The United States was in many ways an accomplice of that persecution, which was led by a particularly virulent form of anti-Catholic and anti-religious Free Masonry, which was introduced into Mexico by an American ambassador in the last century.

In the twentieth century, the persecution of the Church in Mexico became more violent and vicious. In 1925 all Church property was confiscated; all religious services, even those performed in private, were forbidden as criminal acts. Priests and bishops were exiled from the country, and some of those who refused to leave were shot.

In the middle of all this, a young Jesuit, Padre Miguel Pro, came back from his studies in Europe and, in disguise, passed unnoticed into Mexico City. He spent the next two years in a fantastic apostolate combining zeal and courage with an amazing humor in outwitting the police. Since he was young and vivacious and apparently doomed, I guess he decided to go to heaven first class. He performed weddings and baptisms in the park in front of the presidential palace, home of one of the more bitter enemies of the Church, Plutarco Calles. The president, looking out the window, was amused by the picnic going on in his park. It was really Father Pro doing a baptism in a punch bowl. He used many disguises, including those of a police inspector and a drunk. One time, having barely escaped from a house where he had offered Mass, he returned in the disguise of a police inspector and berated the policemen for not having captured Father Pro—real pizazz! In 1927, he was finally captured and, along with his brother, was shot by a firing squad in a police station. Refusing the blindfold, he faced the firing squad with a crucifix in one hand and a rosary in the other, his arms outstretched in the form of a cross. When asked for his final words he said, "May God have mercy on you all. May God bless you. Lord, you know I am innocent. With all my heart I forgive my enemies." As the soldiers lifted their rifles he said with his last breath, "*¡Viva Cristo Rey!*" "Long live Christ the King!"

Was this the tragic end of a generous young man or the victory of a martyr? It has been said that the work of a martyr begins, not ends, the day he dies. I was deeply moved to offer Mass recently at the tomb of Father Miguel Pro in Mexico City. Probably relatively few people in Mexico City could tell you who Plutarco Calles was. The vast majority of people, especially the farmers and the peasants, wouldn't know his name. But they certainly know who Padre Pro was. He is now Blessed Miguel Pro, soon to be declared a saint, I hope. And if the world goes on another thousand years (if we manage not to blow the whole place up), chances are very good that not only in Mexico, but throughout the world, Miguel Pro will still be known, his name sandwiched in between the ancient martyrs and those of the future age. Agnes, Cecelia, Edith Stein, Maximilian Kolbe, Miguel Pro, each one of these people represents innumerable others. Blessed Edith Stein and St. Maximilian Kolbe represent the millions of innocent people who died in World War II.

Outside of the airport in Seoul, Korea, is a huge church built in honor of the Korean martyrs. It is situated on a sea cliff where ten thousand men, women, and children were thrown to their deaths at a single time because of their Catholic faith. This great shrine reminds us that "the blood of the martyrs is the seed of the Church". It reminds us also that God brings good out of evil.

You and I are not likely to be martyred. We have not earned such a glorious fate. But we'll probably die of the things people ordinarily die of—strokes, heart attacks, cancer, getting hit by a car or even—in this crazy world—by a stray bullet. But we will die, and the majority of us will know that we're dying when we're dying. This will give us the same opportunity that the martyr has to surrender ourselves freely to God. The ultimate natural evil of this life is death—it ends our biological existence. It is also the opportunity for the ultimate victory, which is eternal life. St. Paul put it so well, "Death, where is your victory? Death where is your sting?" (1 Cor 15:55). The ultimate evil leads to the ultimate good. Yes, the door to eternity is a low, dark door called death. The corridor to the other side is apparently very short, so short indeed that the very saintly often describe their oncoming death with these words, "The Lord will come for me."

My Redeemer Lives

I spoke to a dear holy soul, a cloistered nun who is very old and dying of cancer. She said, "I'm ready to go. I'm anxious to meet our Lord." That's the answer you need to remember when all falls apart. And it will fall apart. The answer is called faith! "I believe that my Redeemer lives and that I shall see him on the last day" (Job 19:25). Most of the time there is no way to understand or explain the troubles or sorrows of this life. Life is mysterious. But Jesus Christ, by coming into the world, has brought the answer to the mystery of life. It is a practical answer, not a speculative one. Why is life like this? I don't know. When I finally get beyond my Purgatory and I have in sight that reality which Christ called his Father's house, then I will know. The practical answer for now is that I believe and know that my Redeemer lives. In the powerful words of Cardinal Newman:

> The Maker of man, the Wisdom of God, has come, not in strength but in weakness. . . . Instead of wealth, He has come poor; instead of honour, He has come in ignominy; instead of blessedness, He has come to suffer. . . . He . . . has shed His

whole blood in satisfaction [for our sin] when a single drop might have sufficed.

And then Newman prays,

> O Jesus, . . . Thou art still mystery. . . . In spite of Thy [awesome] nature, and the clouds and darkness which surround it, Thou canst think of me with a personal affection. Thou hast died that I might live. . . . [Now] as I adore Thee, O Lover of souls, in Thy humiliation, so will I admire Thee and embrace Thee in Thy infinite and everlasting power.[4]

My Redeemer—your Redeemer—has the right to be called that because he suffered with us as well as for us. God could have saved us in some simpler, less terrible way than subjecting himself to the worst that human beings could do, but he wanted us to know how much he loved us when we are in pain and suffering. Salvation surely did not need to come through the murder of the Messiah. But that's how it came, so we could know, in all sufferings and sorrows of life, that our Creator was also our Redeemer, that he would bring joy out of sorrow, hope out of despair, love out of hate, life out of death, eternity out of time. This is our hope. It alone makes sense.

[4] John Henry Newman, *Discourses to Mixed Congregations*, nos. 302–4, 315, in *The Heart of Newman*, ed. E. Przywara (London: Burns and Oates, 1968), 156–58.

The Remedy That Always Works

There are very few remedies in human experience that always work. In the case of great disappointment and intense sorrows, there is one remedy that works infallibly, so long as this remedy is applied carefully and consistently. This is to get out of yourself and help someone else. Long ago I memorized a line from somewhere, "Save another's soul, and it will save your own." I think that the self-preservation implied in this statement fits in well with our Lord's admonition, "Love your neighbor as yourself." The works of mercy are like so many doses of medication for the wounded heart.

When loved ones are lost or failures plague our efforts, we find it all too appealing to step back into the cave of self-pity and lick our wounds. "Why do we have to think of anybody else? No one thinks about us. Nobody loves me, so I'll love myself, and the world can go its own way."

Such behavior is very appealing when one is deeply hurt, but it is absolutely unhelpful and flies in the face of both the example and the words of Christ. The message of the Gospels is that God loved us when we did not love him. Christ laid down his life for his friends when he knew that they would run out on him. His prophecy of the Passion and its meaning for the salvation of the world—"If I be lifted up, I will draw all things to myself"—signified his unqualified mercy burning in the midst of consuming darkness. His prayer of forgiveness on the Cross—"Father, forgive them for they not know what they do"—is the ultimate expression of precisely what I am speaking of, the remedy to sorrow and failure: merciful love.

You may very well believe (and you may be correct) that your wound caused by the loss of a loved one will never heal. You may be struggling to forgive a wrong and know that you will never be able to forget it, but the example of Christ can draw you out of yourself. The magnificent advice of St. John of the Cross speaks very effectively: "Where there is no love, put love and you will draw love out."

The first step in time of distress is to go back to your duties—to care for those who depend on you. This is often done with considerable reluctance. Depression dogs our steps as we literally drag ourselves around. A voice inside, the voice of the wounded self, cries, "Oh, leave me alone, all of you, and let me grieve or rage." Don't listen to this voice!

The next step is to respond to the special needs of those who are desperate or in grief themselves. If this is the case of a death in the family, one is very wise to look after everyone else, to see that things are properly cared for. I have discovered that inevitably, when I was in great personal distress, I found someone who was worse off than I was, alone, rejected, sick, or dying. I resisted the impulse to care for myself, and I tried to be there for that person. I was probably not much help, and I did myself more good than I did him, yet he was grateful or at least receptive.

Generosity, mercy, courtesy, concern for others, even patience are all ways of fulfilling the counsel of Jesus to love your neighbor as yourself and to be merciful as God is merciful. At times like this our nerves are frayed, and we may snap at someone. Then we should be prepared to apologize—that great act of charity and concern, which we think so little about. What a noble thing it is to see someone who is burdened carry the burdens of others. What is more impressive than the compassion and mercy of those who forgive others while they receive no consolation or mercy themselves?

A Startling Example

As I draw this little book to a close, I think of the great example of my friend Terence Cardinal Cooke, who struggled silently with cancer for almost a decade. My memory recalls a whole kaleidoscope of scenes—him standing in the rain to greet the people after Mass only a week after he received his terminal diagnosis (unbeknown to us all), his patient concern for his critics, his merciful forgiveness of his enemies, his freedom from a vindictive spirit, and his consistent interest in the welfare of those in trouble. His terminal period should have been half as long as it was, his last months should have been a time of gradual deterioration, but he worked consistently for the good of the Church and of all who lived in his sphere of influence. During the last few weeks of his life he divided his time between long periods of prayer and writing letters on very serious issues like life and world peace. He even wrote a letter of consolation to the church of Boston on the death of Cardinal Madeiros.[1]

There was great forgetfulness of self in this very sensitive man. One could not discern his sensitivity in any complaints of his, but rather in his ability to be aware of the feelings of others, to anticipate their needs, and to try to avoid what would be offensive to them. He rarely told you of his sorrows and hurts but quickly and by habit turned his attention

---

[1] See B. Groeschel and T. Weber, *Thy Will Be Done: A Spiritual Portrait of Terence Cardinal Cooke* (New York: Alba House, 1991).

to your needs. I recall this in my last visit to him as he lay dying in his residence. It was a most warm and cheerful meeting, and he dismissed lightly both his present suffering and the hurts of the past. I was hospitalized for heart surgery the next day, and he asked his sister and a close priest friend to be sure to visit me and bring a gift. By this time the Cardinal himself was close to death. All his life he had tried to live by the beatitudes, especially merciful love: "Blessed are the merciful, for they shall obtain mercy."

The example of the life of Terence Cooke, like that of so many servants of God, brings home the fact that charity is the greatest of medicines. It is the medicine of the soul. Merciful love will not only overcome all, it heals all. For those willing to try it, even with hesitation and reluctance, its effects will be lasting and most beneficial.

Another great bishop faced death twice: once being struck by an enemy truck and left by the side of the road, and then being wounded by an assassin's bullet. He wrote about the meaning of merciful love. Pope John Paul, in his letter *On the Mercy of God* (*Dives in Misericordia*), writes: "Jesus Christ taught that man not only receives and experiences the mercy of God, but that he is also called to 'practice mercy' towards others. . . . All the beatitudes . . . indicate the way of conversion and of reform of life, but the one referring to those who are merciful is particularly eloquent in this regard. Man attains to the merciful love of God, His mercy, to the extent that he himself is interiorly transformed in the spirit of that love towards his neighbors." [2]

---

[2] Pope John Paul II, *Dives in Misericordia* (Boston: St. Paul Editions, 1980), 41–42.

Prayers and Thoughts for Dark Times

When one is struggling to go on in dark times and trials, it is often most helpful to cling to a prayer or thought. We are too distracted to think of anything complicated. We need something simple and to the point. The following prayers and thoughts, arranged around the needs we have discussed, may be helpful.

God Is with Me

For God Alone   PSALM 62:5–7
For God alone my soul waits in silence;
    from him comes my salvation.
He only is my rock and my salvation, my fortress;
    I shall not be greatly moved.
On God rests my deliverance and my honor;
    my mighty rock, my refuge is God.
Trust in him at all times, O people; pour out your heart
    before him; God is refuge for us.

Out of the Depths   PSALM 130
Out of the depths I cry to thee, O LORD!
    Lord, hear my voice! Let thy ears be attentive to the
    voice of my supplications!
If thou, O LORD, shouldst mark iniquities,
    Lord, who could stand?
But there is forgiveness with thee,
    that thou mayest be feared.
I wait for the LORD, my soul waits, and in his word I hope;
    my soul waits for the LORD more than watchmen for the
    morning, more than watchmen for the morning.
O Israel, hope in the LORD!
    For with the LORD there is steadfast love,
    and with him is plenteous redemption.
And he will redeem Israel from all his iniquities.

Do Not Be Afraid ISAIAH 41:10–13

Fear not, for I am with you, be not dismayed,
    for I am your God; I will strengthen you,
    I will help you,
    I will uphold you with my victorious right hand.
Behold, all who are incensed against you shall be put to
    shame and confounded; those who strive against you shall
    be as nothing and shall perish.
You shall seek those who contend with you, but you shall
    not find them; those who war against you shall be as
    nothing at all.
For I, the LORD your God, hold your right hand; it is I who
    say to you, "Fear not, I will help you."

Do Not Worry MATTHEW 6:25–33

Therefore I tell you, do not be anxious about your life, what you shall eat or what you shall drink, nor about your body, what you shall put on. Is not life more than food and the body more than clothing? Look at the birds of the air: they neither sow nor reap nor gather into barns, and yet your heavenly Father feeds them. Are you not of more value than they? And which of you by being anxious can add one cubit to his span of life? And why are you anxious about clothing? Consider the lilies of the field, how they grow; they neither toil nor spin; yet I tell you, even Solomon in all his glory was not arrayed like one of these. But if God so clothes the grass of the field, which today is alive and tomorrow is thrown into the oven, will he not much more clothe you, O men of little faith? Therefore do not be anxious, saying, 'What shall we eat?' or 'What shall we drink?' or 'What shall we wear?' For the Gentiles seek all these things; and your heavenly Father knows that you need them all. But seek first his kingdom and his righteousness, and all these things shall be yours as well.

When All Seems Dark

Most High, Glorious God
Most high, glorious God,
lighten the darkness of my heart
and grant me, Lord,
a correct faith,
a certain hope,
a perfect charity,
and sense of knowledge,
so that I may carry out
Your holy and true command.
—St. Francis of Assisi

And Job Said . . . JOB 3:2–6, 20–26
And Job said, "Let the day perish wherein I was born, and
the night which said, 'A man-child is conceived.' Let that
day be darkness! May God above not seek it, nor light shine
upon it. Let gloom and deep darkness claim it. Let clouds
dwell upon it; let the blackness of the day terrify it. That
night—let thick darkness seize it! let it not rejoice among
the days of the year, let it not come into the number of the
months.

"Why is light given to him that is in misery, and life to the
bitter in soul, who long for death and it comes not, and dig
for it more than for hid treasures; who rejoice exceedingly,
and are glad, when they find the grave? Why is light given to
a man whose way is hid, whom God has hedged in? For my
sighing comes as my bread, and my groanings are poured out
like water. For the thing that I fear comes upon me, and
what I dread befalls me. I am not at ease, nor am I quiet; I
have no rest; but trouble comes."

Prayer of One Very Ill

Lord, the day is drawing to a close, and, like all the other days, it leaves with me the impression of utter defeat. I have done nothing for You: neither have I said conscious prayers, nor performed works of charity, nor any work at all, work that is sacred for every Christian who understands its significance. I have not even been able to control that childish impatience and those foolish rancours which so often occupy the place that should be Yours in the "no man's land" of my emotions. It is in vain that I promise You to do better. I shall be no different tomorrow, nor on the day that follows.

When I retrace the course of my life, I am overwhelmed by the same impression of inadequacy. I have sought You in prayer and in service of my neighbour, for we cannot separate You from our brothers any more than we can separate our body from our spirit. But in seeking You, do I not find myself? Do I not wish to satisfy myself? Those works that I secretly termed good and saintly, dissolve in the light of approaching eternity, and I dare no longer lean on these supports that have lost their stability.

Even actual sufferings bring me no joy because I bear them so badly. Perhaps we are all like this: incapable of discerning anything but our own wretchedness and our own despairing cowardice before the light of the Beyond that waxes on our horizon.

But it may be, O Lord, that this impression of privation is part of a divine plan. It may be that in Your eyes, self-complacency is the most obnoxious of all fripperies, and that we must come before You naked so that You, You alone, may clothe us.[1] —MARGUERITE TEILHARD DE CHARDIN

[1] *The Soul Afire*, ed. H. A. Reinhold (New York: Doubleday, Image Books, 1973), 109. Mme de Chardin was foundress of Union of the Sick in France during the 1930s.

Trusting in God

The Sheltering Rock

The huge, unyielding rock that shelters the souls from all storms is the divine will, which is always there, though hidden beneath the veil of trials and the most commonplace actions. Deep within those shadows is the hand of God to support and carry us to complete self-abandonment. And when a soul has arrived at this sublime state it need fear nothing which is said against it, for there is no longer anything for it to say or do in self-defense. Since it is the work of God, we must not try to justify it. Its effects and its consequences will vindicate it enough. There is nothing to be done but let them unfold. If we no longer rely on our own ideas, we must not try to defend ourselves with words, for words can only express our ideas. So, no ideas, no words. What use would they be? To give reasons for our behavior? But we do not know these reasons, for they are hidden in the source of our actions, and from that source we have received only influences we can neither describe nor understand. So we must let the consequences justify themselves. Every link in this divine chain is unbreakable, and the meaning of what has happened earlier is seen in the consequences which follow. The soul no longer lives in a world of thoughts, of imagination, of endless words. Now these no longer occupy it; neither do they nourish or sustain it. It no longer sees where it is going or where it will go. It relies no longer on its own ideas to help it to bear the weariness and difficulties of the journey. It carries on with a profound conviction of its own weakness. But with each step the road widens and, having started, the soul advances along it without hesitation. It is innocent, simple

and faithful and follows the straight path of God's commandments, relying on Him, whom it meets continually
along this path.[2]—Jean-Pierre de Caussade, S.J.

The Silent Guide

When God becomes our guide He insists that we trust Him
without reservations and put aside all nervousness about His
guidance. We are sent along the path He has chosen for us,
but we cannot see it, and nothing we have read is any help
to us. Were we acting on our own we should have to rely
on our experience. It would be too risky to do anything
else. But it is very different when God acts with us. Divine
action is always new and fresh, it never retraces its steps, but
always finds new routes. When we are led by this action,
we have no idea where we are going, for the paths we tread
cannot be discovered from books or by any of our thoughts.
But these paths are always opened in front of us and we are
impelled along them. Imagine we are in a strange district at
night and are crossing fields unmarked by any path, but we
have a guide. He asks no advice nor tells us of his plans. So
what can we do except trust him? It is no use trying to see
where we are, look at maps or question passers-by. That
would not be tolerated by a guide who wants us to rely on
him. He will get satisfaction from overcoming our fears and
doubts, and will insist that we have complete trust in him.

God's activity can never be anything but good, and does
not need to be reformed or controlled. It began at the creation of the world and up to now has continued with the
same energy which knows no limits. Its fertility is inexhaustible. It does one thing today, another tomorrow, yet it
is the same activity which every moment produces con-

---

[2] *Abandonment to Divine Providence*, trans. John Beevers (New York: Doubleday, Image Books, 1975), 109. Several translations are available.

stantly fresh results, and it will continue throughout eternity. It produced Abel, Noah, and Abraham—all different types. Isaac is also original. Jacob is not a duplicate of him, nor is Joseph a facsimile of Jacob. Moses is different from his ancestors. David and the prophets bear no resemblance to the patriarchs. John the Baptist stands alone. Jesus Christ is the first-born, and the Apostles are moved more by guidance of His spirit than by imitating His works. Jesus Christ did not restrict Himself, for He did not follow all His own precepts literally. His most holy soul was always inspired by the Holy Spirit and always responsive to its slightest breath. He never had to consult the moment that had passed to know what to do in the coming one, for His every moment was conditioned by the breath of grace according to those eternal truths contained in the invisible and unfathomable wisdom of the Holy Trinity. His soul received its orders constantly and carried them out in His daily life. The Gospel lets us see the effect of these truths in the life of Jesus Christ, and it is this same Jesus Christ, always alive and active, who continues to live and work fresh wonders in the souls of those who love Him.

If we wish to live according to the Gospel, we must abandon ourselves simply and completely to the action of God. Jesus Christ is its source. He "is the same today as He was yesterday and as He will be forever" (Heb 13:8). What He has done is finished, what remains to be done is being carried on every moment. Every saint shares in this divine life, and Jesus Christ, though always the same, is different in each one. The life of each saint is the life of Jesus Christ. It is a new gospel.[3] —JEAN-PIERRE DE CAUSSADE, S.J.

---

[3] *Abandonment to Divine Providence*, 83–84.

I Can Not Be Thrown Away

1. God was all-complete, all-blessed in Himself; but it was His will to create a world for His glory. He is Almighty, and might have done all things Himself, but it has been His will to bring about His purposes by the beings He has created. We are all created to His glory—we are created to do His will. I am created to do something or to be something for which no one else is created; I have a place in God's counsels, in God's world, which no one else has; whether I be rich or poor, despised or esteemed by man, God knows me and calls me by my name.

2. God has created me to do Him some definite service; He has committed some work to me which He has not committed to another. I have my mission—I never may know it in this life, but I shall be told it in the next. Somehow I am necessary for His purposes, as necessary in my place as an Archangel in his—if, indeed, I fail, He can raise another, as He could make the stones children of Abraham. Yet I have a part in this great work; I am a link in a chain, a bond of connexion between persons. He has not created me for naught. I shall do good, I shall do His work; I shall be an angel of peace, a preacher of truth in my own place, while not intending it, if I do but keep His commandments and serve Him in my calling.

3. Therefore I will trust Him. Whatever, wherever I am, I can never be thrown away. If I am in sickness, my sickness may serve Him; in perplexity, my perplexity may serve Him; if I am in sorrow, my sorrow may serve Him. My sickness, or perplexity, or sorrow may be necessary causes of some great end, which is quite beyond us. He does nothing in vain; He may prolong my life, He may shorten it; He knows what He is about. He may take away my friends, He may throw me among strangers, He may make me feel desolate,

make my spirits sink, hide the future from me—still He knows what He is about.

O Adonai, O Ruler of Israel, Thou that guidedst Joseph like a flock, O Emmanuel, O Sapientia, I give myself to Thee. I trust Thee wholly. Thou art wiser than I—more loving to me than I myself. Deign to fulfil Thy high purposes in me whatever they be—work in and through me. I am born to serve Thee, to be Thine, to be Thy instrument. Let me be Thy blind instrument. I ask not to see—I ask not to know—I ask simply to be used.[4]

—JOHN HENRY CARDINAL NEWMAN

Prayers in Time of Sickness

I Must in a Little Time Go to God
A letter written in old age

I do not pray that you may be delivered from your pains, but I pray God earnestly that He would give you strength and patience to bear them as long as He pleases. Comfort yourself with Him who holds you fastened to the cross. He will loose you when He thinks fit. Happy those who suffer with Him. Accustom yourself to suffer in that manner, and seek from Him the strength to endure as much, and as long, as He shall judge to be necessary for you. The men of the world do not comprehend these truths, nor is it to be wondered at, since they suffer like what they are, and not like Christians. They consider sickness as a pain to nature, and not as a favor from God; and seeing it only in that light, they find nothing in it but grief and distress. But those who consider sickness as

---

[4] Meditations on Christian Doctrine, 1, in *Prayers, Verses, and Devotions* (San Francisco: Ignatius Press, 1989), 338–39. This prayer was written in 1848, when Newman experienced many failures and misunderstandings.

coming from the hand of God, as the effect of His mercy, and the means which He employs for their salvation—such commonly find in it great sweetness and sensible consolation.

I wish you could convince yourself that God is often (in some sense) nearer to us, and more effectually present with us, in sickness than in health. Rely upon no other physician; for, according to my apprehension, He reserves your cure to Himself. Put, then, all your trust in Him, and you will soon find the effects of it in your recovery, which we often retard by putting greater confidence in physic than in God.

Whatever remedies you make use of, they will succeed only so far as He permits. When pains come from God, He only can cure them. He often sends diseases of the body to cure those of the soul. Comfort yourself with the sovereign Physician both of the soul and body.

Be satisfied with the condition in which God places you: however happy you may think me, I envy you. Pains and sufferings would be a paradise to me while I should suffer with my God, and the greatest pleasures would be hell to me if I could relish them without Him. All my consolation would be to suffer something for His sake.

I must in a little time, go to God. What comforts me in this life is that I now see Him by faith; and I see Him in such a manner as might make me say sometimes, *I believe no more, but I see*. I feel what faith teaches us, and in that assurance and that practice of faith I will live and die with Him.

Continue, then always with God; it is the only support and comfort for your affliction. I shall beseech Him to be with you. I present my service.[5] —BROTHER LAWRENCE

[5] *The Practice of the Presence of God*, letter 11 (Old Tappan, N.J.: Fleming H. Revell, Spire Book, n.d.), 55–57. Many editions are available. Brother Lawrence, a seventeenth-century French Carmelite lay brother, gave us many beautiful sayings on trust in God, highly valued in the literature of spirituality.

Prayers of a Shepherd of Souls
Attributed to Terence Cardinal Cooke [6]

FOR A SICK PERSON

Almighty God, giver of health and healing, grant to Your servant a palpable sense of Your presence and perfect trust in You. In suffering may he cast his care on You, so that, enfolded in Your love and power, he may receive health and salvation according to Your gracious will. Through Christ our Lord. Amen.

FOR ONE'S SELF WHEN ILL

Dear Lord, You are the greatest physician. I turn to You in my sickness and ask You to help me. Put Your hand upon me as You did for the people long ago and let health and wholeness come into me from You. I put myself under Your care and affirm my faith that even now Your marvelous healing grace is making me well and strong again.

I know that I ask more than I deserve, but You never measure our benefits on that basis. You just love us back into health. Do that for me. I earnestly ask and I will try to serve You more faithfully. This I promise through Christ our Lord. Amen.

PRAYER WHEN WORRIED

Dear Lord, I'm worried and full of fear. Anxiety and apprehension fill my mind. Could it be that my love for You is weak and imperfect and as a result I am plagued by worry?

---

[6] Terence Cardinal Cooke, *Prayers for Today*, 2nd ed. (New York: Alba House, 1991), 55ff. These prayers were found in an anthology the Cardinal published; and as they are not credited to someone else, they are assumed to be his own.

I have tried to reassure myself that there is nothing to worry about. But such reassurances do not seem to help. I know that I should just rest myself confidently on Your loving care and guidance. But I have been too upset even to pray. Touch me, dear Lord, with Your peace, and help my disturbed spirit to know that You are God and that I need fear no evil.

BEFORE AN OPERATION

Loving Father, I entrust myself to Your care this day; guide with wisdom and skill the minds and hands of those who heal in Your name. Grant that with every cause of illness removed, I may be restored to sound health and learn to live in more perfect harmony with You and with my neighbor. Through Jesus Christ. Amen.

AFTER AN OPERATION

Blessed Savior, I thank You that this operation is safely past and now I rest in Your abiding presence, relaxing every tension, releasing every care and anxiety, receiving more and more of Your healing life into every part of my being. In moments of pain I turn to You for strength; in times of loneliness I feel Your loving nearness. Grant then that Your life and love and joy may flow through me for healing of others in Your name. Amen.

FOR THE APPREHENSIVE PATIENT

Christ said to His loved ones: "I am with you, fear not, be not anxious." May I be confident that, in the trials and crosses of my life, You, O Lord, will be my constant companion. Whenever I cannot stand, You will carry me lovingly in Your arms.

May I have no fear of what may happen tomorrow. For

the same eternal Father who cares for me today will take care of me tomorrow and every day of my life. You, O Lord, will either shield me from suffering or give me strength to bear it patiently. May I be at peace, then, and put aside all useless thoughts, anxieties, and worries. Amen.

FOR THE DEPRESSED PATIENT

Praise to You, O Christ, and honor and glory! As Your Passion drew nearer, You began to know weariness and depression. Thus You took upon Yourself the weakness of our human nature that You might strengthen and console those who are fearful of serious illness. I beg You to free me from all discouragement and anxiety. Grant that all I endure may be to Your glory and for the pardon of my sins. Deliver me from faintheartedness and all unreasonable fears, and fix my heart firmly and unwaveringly on You. Amen.

The Changeless Friend

The Friendship of Jesus

Alone I was, without a single friend to give me a word of encouragement, I could neither pray nor read, but there I remained, for hours and hours together, uneasy in mind and afflicted in spirit, on account of the weight of my trouble, and of the fear that perhaps after all I was being tricked by the devil, and wondering what in the world I could do for my relief. Not a gleam of hope seemed to shine upon me from either earth or heaven; except just this that in the midst of all my fears and dangers I never forgot how Our Lord must be seeing the weight of all I endured.

O my Lord Jesus Christ! What a true friend You are, and how powerful! For when You wish to be with us You can be, and You always do wish it if only we will receive You. May everything created, O Lord of all the world, praise You and bless You! If only I could tramp the whole world over, proclaiming everywhere with all the strength that is in me what a faithful friend You are to those who will be friends with You! My dear Lord, all else fails and passes away; You, the Lord of them all, never fail, never pass away. What You allow those who love You to suffer is all too little. O my Lord, how kindly, how nobly, how tenderly, how sweetly, You succeed in handling and making sure of Your own! Oh, if only one could secure that one would love nothing but just You alone! You seem, my dear Lord, to put to the trial with rods and agonies one who loves You, only that, just when You have brought her to the last extreme of endurance, she may understand all the more the boundless limits of Your love.[7]

—St. Teresa of Avila

The Little Way of Love

"In the time of the law of fear, before the coming of our Lord, the prophet Isaias, speaking in the name of the King of Heaven, could say: 'Can a mother forget her child? Yet if she should forget, yet will not forget you.' What ecstasy in that promise! Ah! and we would live under the law of love, how can we fail to put to profit the loving advances our Spouse makes to us? How can we fear One 'who lets Himself be held by a hair of her neck'? So we must learn to hold Him prisoner, this God who makes Himself a mendicant for our love. In telling us that a hair can work so great a marvel, He is showing that the *smallest actions* done for love are the actions which win His heart. Ah! if we had to do great

---

[7] *Autobiography*, chap. 15. Quoted in Archbishop Alban Goodier, *The Life That Is Light* (London: Burns and Oates, 1935), 67.

things, how much to be pitied we should be! . . . But how fortunate we are, since Jesus lets Himself be held by the *smallest!*" [8] —St. Thérèse of Lisieux

With Empty Hands
A prayer to Christ Crucified

I come before You with empty hands, all the secret store of grace I fling into needy hearts, crying in the bitter night of fear and loneliness. Spendthrift of Your love, I keep before me Your empty Hands—empty and riven with the great nails hollowing out rivers of mercy, until all Your substance was poured out. So, I, my Jesus, with hands emptied for Your love, stand confident before Your Cross, love's crimson emblem. It is the empty who are filled: those who have made themselves spendthrifts for You alone, fill the last of Your brethren while they themselves are nourished by Your Love, more and more emptied that they may be filled with You. [9]

—St. Thérèse of Lisieux

A Parable of the Cross

All the people who had ever lived were assembled before the throne of God. They were a sullen lot. They all had complaints, and they began to murmur among themselves. Who does God think He is, anyway?

One of the groups was composed of Jews who had suffered persecution. Some had died in gas chambers and con-

---

[8] *Collected Letters of St. Thérèse of Lisieux*, letter of July 12, 1896, ed. André Combes, trans. Frank Sheed (London: Sheed & Ward, 1949), 275–76. St. Thérèse, a nineteenth-century French Carmelite nun, informally taught "a little Way of Love" as the road to God. She wrote this letter to her sister Léonie.

[9] Prayer card: Sr. Teresa of the Trinity, "Meditations Based on Writings of St. Thérèse of Lisieux" (Carmel of Terre Haute, Ind.).

centration camps—and they grumbled; how could God know of the suffering they had been through? Another group was slaves—black men and women with brands on their brows, great hosts of them, who had suffered indignities at the hands of those who called themselves "God's people"—What could God know about their plight? There were long lines of refugees driven from their lands—homeless people, who had nowhere to lay their heads. And there were poor people, who had never on this earth been able to make ends meet. There were sick ones and sufferers of all kinds, hundreds of groups, each with a complaint against God. What could He know what human beings were forced to endure?

From each group a leader was chosen and a commission appointed to draw up the case against the Almighty Himself. Instead of God judging them, they began judging Him. And the verdict was that God should be sentenced to live on earth as a human being with no safeguards to protect His divinity. And here was a bill of particulars:

Let Him be born a Jew. Let Him be born poor. Let even the legitimacy of His birth be suspect. Give Him hard work to do and poverty that He might know the pinch. Let Him be rejected by His people. Give Him for friends only those who are held in contempt. Let Him be betrayed by one of His friends. Let Him be indicted on false charges, tried before a prejudiced jury, convicted by a cowardly judge. Let Him be abandoned by His friends and see what it is to be terribly alone. Let Him be tortured, and then let Him die at the hands of His enemies.

As each group announced its sentence on God, roars of approval went up from the throng. When the last had finished, the raucous noise had become almost deafening . . . and then everyone turned toward the throne. And suddenly heaven was filled with shocked penitent silence. For where there had been a throne, now could be seen a Cross.[10]

—ANDREW ARMSTRONG

Finding Rest in Christ
We Are to Rest in God above All Goods and Gifts

DISCIPLE: Above all things, and in all things, do thou, my soul, rest always in the Lord, for He is the eternal rest of the saints.

Give me, O most sweet and loving Jesus, to repose in Thee above all things created; above all health and beauty, above all glory and honor, above all power and dignity, above all knowledge and subtlety, above all riches and arts, above all joy and gladness, above all fame and praise, above all sweetness and consolation, above all hope and promise, above all merit and desire.

Above all the gifts and presents that Thou canst give and infuse, above all the joy and jubilation that the mind can contain and experience.

In fine, above angels and archangels, and all the hosts of heaven, above all things visible and invisible, and above all that which is less than Thee, my God!

For Thou, O Lord, my God! art the best above all things. Thou alone most high; Thou alone most powerful; Thou alone most sufficient and most full; Thou alone most sweet and most comforting.

Thou alone most beautiful and most loving; Thou alone most noble and most glorious above all things; in whom all things are found together in all their perfection, and always have been and always will be.

---

[10] I have been unable to discover any information about the author, but surely a Christian capable of writing this will rejoice to have it shared.—BJG.

And, therefore, whatever Thou bestowest upon me that is not Thyself, or whatever Thou revealest to me concerning Thyself, or promisest, as long as I see Thee not, nor fully enjoy Thee, is too little and insufficient.

Because, indeed, my heart cannot truly rest, nor be entirely contented, till it rest in Thee, and rise above all Thy gifts and all things created.

O Christ Jesus, most pure lover, Lord of the whole creation, who will give me the wings of true liberty to fly and repose in Thee?—see Ps 55:6(54:7).

Oh, when shall it be fully granted me to attend at leisure, and see how sweet Thou art, O Lord, my God?—Ps 34:8 (33:9).

When shall I fully recollect myself in Thee, that through the love of Thee I may not feel myself, but Thee alone, above all feeling and measure in a manner not known at all?

But now I often sigh and bear my misfortune with grief. Because I meet with many evils in this vale of miseries, which frequently disturb me, afflict me, and cast a cloud over me; often hinder and distract me, allure and entangle me, so that I cannot have free access to Thee, nor enjoy Thy sweet embraces, which are ever enjoyed by blessed spirits.

O Jesus! the brightness of eternal glory, the comfort of a soul in its pilgrimage, my tongue cannot express the sentiments of my heart, but my silence itself speaks to Thee.

How long doth my Lord delay to come?

Let Him come to me, His poor servant, and make me joyful; let Him stretch forth His hand, and deliver me, a wretch, from all anguish.—Ps 138:7(137:7).

Oh, come, oh, come—Rev 22:20, for without Thee I can never have one joyful day, nor hour, for Thou art my joy, and without Thee my table is empty.

I am miserable, and in a manner imprisoned, and loaded

with fetters, till Thou comfortest me with the light of Thy presence, and restorest me to liberty and showest me a favorable countenance.

Let others seek instead of Thee, whatever else pleases them; nothing else doth please me or shall please me, but Thou my God, my hope, my eternal salvation.

I will not hold my peace, nor cease to pray, till Thy grace returns and Thou speakest to me interiorly.

CHRIST. Behold here I am, behold I come to thee, because thou hast called upon Me. Thy tears and the desire of thy soul, thy humiliation and contrition of heart have inclined and brought Me to thee.—Is 38:5.

DISCIPLE. And I said, O Lord, I have called upon Thee and have desired to enjoy Thee, and am ready to renounce all things for Thee.

For Thou didst first stir me up that I might seek Thee.

Be Thou, therefore, blessed. O Lord, who hast showed this goodness to Thy servant, according to the multitude of Thy mercies.

What hath Thy servant more to say in Thy presence, but to humble himself exceedingly before Thee, always remembering his own iniquity and vileness.

For there is none like to Thee amongst all things that are wonderful in heaven or on earth.—Ps 86:8(85:8).

Thy works are exceedingly good, Thy judgements are true and by Thy providence all things are ruled.

Praise, therefore, and glory be to Thee, O wisdom of the Father! Let my tongue, my soul, and all things created join in praising and blessing Thee.[11] —THOMAS À KEMPIS

[11] *Imitation of Christ*, book III, chap. 21. In *Thomas à Kempis* (Brooklyn, N.Y.: Confraternity of the Precious Blood, 1954), 230–31. Several translations are available. This great spiritual classic has fallen out of favor because of its style and uncompromising spirituality. Much good can still be found in it.

The Mercy of God

Psalm 57:1–3

Be merciful to me, O God, be merciful to me, for in thee
    my soul takes refuge; in the shadow of thy wings I will
    take refuge, till the storms of destruction pass by.
I cry to God Most High, to God who fulfils his purpose for me.
He will send from heaven and save me, he will put to
    shame those who trample upon me. God will send forth
    his steadfast love and his faithfulness.

Psalm 143:1–8

Hear my prayer, O LORD; give ear to my supplications!
    In thy faithfulness answer me, in thy righteousness!
Enter not into judgment with thy servant;
    for no man living is righteous before thee.
For the enemy has pursued me; he has crushed my life to
    the ground; he has made me sit in darkness like those
    long dead.
Therefore my spirit faints within me; my heart within me is
    appalled.
I remember the days of old, I meditate on all that thou hast
    done; I muse on what thy hands have wrought.
I stretch out my hands to thee; my soul thirsts for thee like a
    parched land.
Make haste to answer me, O LORD! My spirit fails! Hide not
    thy face from me, lest I be like those who go down to
    the Pit.
Let me hear in the morning of thy steadfast love,
    for in thee I put my trust.
Teach me the way I should go,
    for to thee I lift up my soul.

Wisdom 15:1–3

But thou, our God, art kind and true, patient and ruling all
   things in mercy.

For even if we sin we are thine, knowing thy power; but
   we will not sin, because we know that we are accounted
   thine.

For to know thee is complete righteousness, and to know
   thy power is the root of immortality.

Prayer of Trust

I fly to Your mercy, Compassionate God, who alone are
good. Although my misery is great, and my offenses are
many, I trust in Your mercy, because You are the God of
mercy; and from time immemorial, it has never been heard
of, nor do heaven or earth remember, that a soul trusting in
Your mercy has been disappointed.

O God of compassion, You alone can justify me, and You
will never reject me when I, contrite, approach Your merciful Heart, where no one has ever been refused even if he
were the greatest sinner.[12]—BLESSED FAUSTINA KOWALSKA

We Know Not What Is Good for Us

Ah, Lord, we know not what is good for us, and what is
bad. We cannot foretell the future, nor do we know when
Thou comest to visit us, in what form Thou wilt come.
And therefore, we leave it all to Thee. Do Thou Thy good
pleasure to us and in us. Let us ever look at Thee, and do
Thou look upon us, and give us the grace of Thy bitter
Cross and Passion, and console us in Thy own way and at
Thy own time.[13]—JOHN HENRY CARDINAL NEWMAN

[12] *Jesus, I Trust in You* (Krakow, Poland: Shrine of the Divine Mercy, 1994),
62. Blessed Faustina Kowalska (20th cent.) was a Polish lay sister and mystic.

[13] Quoted in Erich Przywara, S.J., *The Heart of Newman* (London: Burns
and Oates, 1963), 197.

At the Death of a Loved One

They Do Not Forget Us

Not long after our conversion and regeneration by Your baptism, You took him from this life, by then a baptized Catholic and serving You in Africa in perfect chastity among his own people, for he had made his whole family Christian. And now he lives in Abraham's bosom. Whatever is meant by that bosom, there my Nebridius lives, my most beloved friend, Your son by adoption and no longer a freed-man only. There he lives. For what other place is there for such a soul? There he lives, in the place of which he asked me, an ignorant poor creature, so many questions. He no longer puts his bodily ear to my lips, but the lips of his spirit to Your fountain, drinking his fill of wisdom, all that his thirst requires, happy without end. Nor do I think he is so intoxicated with the draught of that wisdom as to forget me, since You, O Lord of whom he drinks, are mindful of all.[14] —St. Augustine

Looking Ahead

For many a century before Christ, many a millennium perhaps, that was the established view—survival a misery of mere existence. So the Old Testament Jews felt; so felt the great Greeks.

But not I. Christ has told us that He has gone to prepare a place for us, that where He is we may be. His word of welcome when we arrive there will be "Enter into the joy of my Father." Is the detail of the joy beyond present com-

---

[14] *Confessions*, book IX, chap. 3, trans. Frank Sheed (New York: Sheed & Ward, 1942).

prehension? I should hope so. I don't want to stay retarded at my present level.

But God will be there, at last seen with direct vision; Christ will be there and his Mother and all who have not refused Him. For those I have loved here I shall have a love with no dross in it; the joy I have had in them here I shall have there, unclouded.

There is one small matter peculiar to myself. I have written so much about the Trinity: Will the sight of Father, Son and Holy Spirit make me wish that I could get back to earth and tear that writing all up? I also feel a special uncertainty about meeting St. Augustine, whose *Confessions* I translated. I can only hope he thinks better of my translation than I do. But perhaps, by now he may think his own book pretty bad, and my translation not much worse.

I know, for I have seen, that as death approaches, there is a diminishing of the flow of energy from soul to body, a loosening of the bond between them, an unease that can give rise to real anguish. I hope that when that time comes a priest will be there to hear my sins and in Christ's name absolve me and give me the Blessed Eucharist (which the Church pleasantly calls *viaticum*, supplies for the journey) and anoint me, anoint especially the sense through which from the beginning of life the world has poured in on me.

But with all this, I can't conceive a future life without a possibility of cleansing (which is what the word purgatory means)—not because I deserve it, but because I need it. The thought of entering the presence of the all-pure God as the spotted object that I am revolts me. There are the elements of self unsurrendered—me still wanting what I want just because I want it. Healing is a better word than cleansing. My will needs straightening; and that cannot be done without pain—not penal pain, pain in the sheer forcing of the will away from habits grown into second nature. Here or hereafter, with God's aid I must will my own will straight. He will help me to do it. But He won't do it for me.

I hardly ever meet anyone who wants to go to heaven. I do. Yet not at once. Not today. Next week, perhaps.

So there is a shrinking. Clearly I am a puzzle I have not completely solved.[15] —FRANK SHEED

The Farewell of the Christian Community

Dear brother (sister), I commend you to almighty God, and entrust you to Him who created you, so that, when by your dying you have paid the debt to which every man is subject, you may return to your maker, to Him who formed you from the clay of the earth. Then, when your soul goes forth from your body, may the radiant company of angels come to meet you. May the assembly of the apostles, our judges, welcome you. May the victorious army of white-robed martyrs meet you on your way. May the glittering throng of confessors, bright as lilies, gather about you. May the glorious choir of virgins receive you. May the patriarchs enfold you in the embrace of blessed peace. May St. Joseph, beloved patron of the dying, raise you high in hope, and may the holy Mother of God, the Virgin Mary, lovingly turn her eyes toward you. And then, gentle and joyful, may Christ Jesus appear before you, to assign you a place forever among those who stand in His presence. May Christ, who was crucified for your sake, free you from excruciating pain. May Christ, who died for you, free you from the death that never ends. May Christ, the Son of the living God, set you in the ever-green loveliness of his paradise, and may He, the

[15] *Death into Life* (New York: Arena Lettres, 1977), 132-34. Frank Sheed (d. 1981) was a great Catholic apologist.

true Shepherd, recognize you as one of His own. May He free you from all your sins and assign you a place at His right hand in the company of His elect. May you see your Redeemer face to face and, standing in His presence forever, may you see with joyful eyes Truth revealed in all its fulness. And so, having taken your place in the ranks of the Blessed, may you enjoy the happiness of divine contemplation for ever and ever. Amen.[16] —*The Roman Ritual*

Prayer for the Departing Soul

O Lord Jesus Christ, You said through the mouth of the prophet, "I have loved you with an everlasting love: therefore in pity have I drawn you to Myself." Deign, I implore You, to offer up and show to God, the Father almighty, on behalf of Your servant, N., that love of Yours which drew You down from heaven to earth to endure all Your bitter sufferings. Deliver him (her) from all the pains and sufferings which he (she) fears that he (she) deserves for his (her) sins. and grant salvation to his (her) soul in this hour when it takes its departure. Open to him (her) the gates of life, and cause him (her) to rejoice with Your saints in everlasting glory. And do You, most loving Lord Jesus Christ, who redeemed us by Your most precious blood, take pity on the soul of this Your servant, N., and lead him (her) into the lovely places of paradise that are forever green so that he (she) may live with You in undivided love, never to be separated from You and from those whom You chose. You who with the Father and the Holy Spirit live and reign, God, for ever and ever. Amen.[17] —*The Roman Ritual*

---

[16] "Recommendation of a Departing Soul", *Collectio Rituum* (The Roman Ritual) (New York: Benziger Brothers, 1964), 204.

[17] Ibid., 211.

Prayer for One Who Has Taken His Own Life

Crucified Savior, there is no place for me to go but to the foot of Your Cross. I feel desolation, defeat, betrayal, rejection. I tried. I tried to stop the flood, to calm the earthquake, to put out the raging fire. I did not even know how desperate it all was. There is absolutely no consolation, no answer, no softening of my grief. It is complete darkness. I grieve for my dear friend [or relative], for what was and what could have been. Is life so awful that all struggle had to end, that defeat was inevitable? There is nothing but silence outside and screaming inside. I know that the wound will heal, but now I don't even want it to. I know that there will be a huge scar in its place. That scar will be all that I have left.

I am filled with terror for the one I loved and cared for. Salvation. If only I was certain of salvation for the one who is gone, defeated by this life. There is no one I can come to but You—Crucified One. Your prayer of dereliction, which always puzzled me before, now is the only thing with any meaning at all. I put my dear one whose body is destroyed into Your hands. Reach down from the Cross and embrace this wounded and broken soul. You descended into hell. Find our friend on the edge and rescue the one who has gone from us. We have no place to go in the world, in the whole universe but here to You, to Your cross—it is our only hope. Into Your hands, O Lord, we commend this spirit. Amen.[18]

---

[18] The death of a loved one by suicide is one of the most appalling experiences one can endure. There is an anguish comprehended only by those who have experienced it. Since I lived through a suicide long ago, I write this prayer just for those who know. Although this disturbed young man took his life many years ago, when his girlfriend rejected him, the gunshot still echoes through my mind.—BJG.

Prayers for the Bystanders at the Grave

I.

Let us pray.

Grant, O Lord, we pray You, that while we lament the departure of our brother (sister), Your servant, out of this life, we may bear in mind that we are most certainly to follow him (her). Give us the grace to make ready for that last hour by a devout and holy life, and protect us against a sudden and unprovided death. Teach us how to watch and pray, so that when Your summons comes, we may go forth to meet the Bridegroom and enter with Him into life everlasting. Through Christ our Lord. Amen.

II.

Let us pray.

Almighty and most merciful Father, you know the weakness of our nature. Bow down Your ear in pity to Your servants, upon whom You have laid the heavy burden of sorrow. Take away out of their hearts the spirit of rebellion, and teach them to see Your good and gracious purpose working in all the trials which You sent upon them. Grant that they may not languish in fruitless and unavailing grief, nor sorrow as those who have no hope, but through their tears look meekly up to You, the God of all consolation. Through Christ our Lord. Amen.[19] —*The Roman Ritual*

In Paradisium

May the angels lead you into paradise; may the martyrs come to welcome you on your way, and lead you into the holy city, Jerusalem. May the choir of angels welcome you and with Lazarus who once was poor may you have everlasting rest.[20] —*The Roman Ritual*

---

[19] *Collectio Rituum* (The Roman Ritual), 256.
[20] Ibid., 246.

Suggested Readings

Many books have been written for people going through times of trial. Along with the works already mentioned in this book, the following seem to me to be very helpful.

A beautiful and powerful statement on the meaning of suffering is given by Pope John Paul II in his apostolic letter *On the Christian Meaning of Human Suffering* (*Salvifici Dolores*) given in February 1984, available through St. Paul Editions, Boston, Mass. My friend Peter Kreeft has written one of his penetrating books on the subject: *Making Sense Out of Suffering* (Ann Arbor, Mich.: Servant Books, 1986).

François Varillon's *The Humility and Suffering of God* (New York: Alba House, 1983) tells us much about what we can know about God's side of the story. I have always found Romano Guardini's *The Lord* (New York: Regnery, 1954) most enlightening and moving. St. Thomas More's *The Sadness of Christ* (Princeton, N.J.: Scepter, 1993) is a powerful meditation, as are a number of books and tapes of Bishop Fulton J. Sheen.

One of the commonly mentioned books on the subject is *When Bad Things Happen to Good People* (New York: Avon, 1983) by Rabbi Harold S. Kushner. This sensitive book by a compassionate man brings his experience of the Jewish Scriptures into focus, although Rabbi Kushner mentions the unique perspective that the sufferings of Jesus must give to the struggles of the Christian. Somewhat in response to this work is a book by Bartholomew Gottemoller, a Trappist monk, entitled *Why Good People Suffer* (New York: Vantage

Press, 1987). Another book, *Where Is God When You Need Him?* (New York: Alba House, 1992), by Karl Schultz, brings together the story of Job and the teaching of Jesus in a helpful and meditative way.

When all is said and done, the most powerful things ever written about suffering, sorrow, and death are in the Sacred Scriptures. This is why every year during Holy Week the Church brings us through the solemn commemoration of the Passion, Death, and Resurrection of our Lord Jesus Christ.

Index